D0410577

MAKING CUPCAKES WITH

LOLA

MAKING CUPCAKES WITH
LOLA

VICTORIA JOSSEL & ROMY LEWIS OF LOLA'S

photography by Kate Whitaker

RYLAND
PETERS
& SMALL
LONDON NEW YORK

Senior designer Megan Smith
Commissioning editor Céline Hughes
Production Gordana Simakovic
Art director Leslie Harrington
Publishing director Alison Starling

Food stylist Lucy McKelvie
Prop stylist Liz Belton
Indexer Hilary Bird

First published in the United Kingdom
in 2011 by Ryland Peters & Small
20–21 Jockey's Fields
London WC1R 4BW
and
519 Broadway, 5th Floor
New York NY 10012
www.rylandpeters.com

10 9 8 7 6 5 4 3 2 1

Text © Victoria Jossel and Romy Lewis
2011
Design and photographs
© Ryland Peters & Small 2011

ISBN: 978-1-84975-186-5

Printed and bound in China

CIP data from the Library of Congress
has been applied for.

A CIP record for this book is available
from the British Library.

NOTES
• All spoon measurements are level,
unless otherwise specified.
• Ovens should be preheated to the
specified temperature. Recipes in this
book were tested using a regular oven.
If using a convection oven, follow the
manufacturer's instructions for adjusting
temperatures.
• All eggs are medium, unless otherwise
specified. Recipes containing raw or
partially cooked egg should not be
served to the very young, very old,
anyone with a compromised immune
system or pregnant women.
• When using the zest of citrus fruit in,
try to find organic or unwaxed fruits and
wash well before using. If you can find
only treated fruit, scrub well in warm
soapy water and rinse.
• All butter is unsalted, unless otherwise
specified.
• The cupcake cases used throughout
the book are large. It is recommended
that muffin-sized cases be used.

DEDICATION
Romy
To my grandfather, Stanley, whose memory remains an inspiration, and to
my parents for their belief in me.
'I have always worked with a team of people that has inspired me to input
to the best of my ability and motivated me.' Stanley Lewis.

Victoria
This book is dedicated to my wonderful husband. Your encouragement, support,
unconditional love and endless advice made LOLA's a reality. You are my inspiration
and I can't wait to share with you the joy our baby boy will bring.

CONTENTS

INTRODUCTION

In the beginning we had nothing but an idea, ambition and a box of empty cupcake cases. We lived across the road from each other and started baking in our mothers' kitchens, taking orders in our bedrooms and making deliveries in our cars. There really was no written recipe for us to follow; a combination of the right timing, some good luck and two incredibly determined minds meant things evolved quickly and organically. Within a year we managed to fill the empty cupcake cases, move out of our home kitchens and set up a LOLA's production bakery in Primrose Hill, London.

Life before LOLA's was very different. You would have found Victoria at her desk at Goldman Sachs where she worked as part of the Credit Derivatives team. After five years, Victoria decided to trade her knowledge of finance systems to explore her more creative side in the cupcake market, which was starting to establish itself in the UK. She had the idea of setting up a cupcake company and when orders started rolling in, she asked a family friend, Romy, to join her. Romy had recently graduated with a degree in Broadcast Journalism. Her passion for journalism and frontline reporting was sidelined when she was presented with this new opportunity. The risk and excitement associated with starting a new business from nothing was adrenaline-inducing enough to satisfy Romy and the two became partners. The business became official in September 2006 and LOLA's was born.

We're both from very relaxed and warm South African families who love entertaining. It took us a while to realize that this was the inspiration behind LOLA's. When we began, our knowledge of the science required in baking was minimal. As a result, we learned a lot in a very short space of time and we called on all of our resources to help. We tried and tested hundreds of recipes and methods before we mastered LOLA's signature taste and unique style: uncomplicated yet sophisticated.

Our motto was simple: to handcraft the best cupcakes that you have ever tasted. And we hold ourselves to this standard every single day. To achieve this goal, we source the finest ingredients to ensure that the freshness and quality of our product is never compromised. Fortunately we now have a team of specialist bakers and decorators who continue to amaze us every day with their creativity, passion and skill. We always remain true to our mission statement, which states that we 'believe in preserving the quality of freshly baked cakes in a world where all things natural and simple have been replaced by complexity and obscure chemicals'.

We have an obsessive attention to detail and never compromise on taste or quality. Our goal is to show each and every customer LOLA's wow factor. Whether you make your purchase in one of our stores, online or over the phone, our wonderful team in the office and our store retail assistants are trained to leave you

'When we discovered LOLA's back in 2007, it was such an exciting moment for Selfridges. The cupcakes were a revelation – wondrous colours and flavours. LOLA's is a vibrant brand driven by passionate foodies Victoria and Romy. We look forward to their continued success.'

Ewan Venters, Food Director, Selfridges & Co

OR
ORE
BUT

PEA
HOM
SMO

RO
MAR
IN M

STR
PUR

feeling uplifted from having been a part of the LOLA's experience.

We have expanded our retail outlets across central London and today have our own standalone store in Mayfair, which we refer to as 'LOLA's Personal Touch', and concessions in Selfridges, Topshop and an outlet in Harrods, as well as our online store, which helped us get the business off the ground on Day One.

We leave nothing to the imagination; our daily range consists of 17 different flavours and our talented product developer spends months coming up with enchanting and innovative creations. We have extended our range to include everything from personalized and bespoke cupcakes, to themed cupcakes – and our ideas don't stop there. From dinner-party tables, through airport security, on your wedding cake stand or on the boardroom table, LOLA's has the perfect cupcakes, whatever the occasion.

Like any business, LOLA's comes with its challenges. On a super-busy day our team might make up to 7,000 cupcakes and 60 large cakes. Every day is different and we're always looking at what we can do next to ensure we stay ahead of the trends in such a competitive market. The most challenging part of our job is trying to be on top of everything. Not only do we need to understand how to bake and decorate the perfect cupcake, we've also had to learn how to be accountants, lawyers, psychologists, HR specialists, marketing and branding professionals, building surveyors, customer service experts – and the list goes on! However, LOLA's continues to be the most incredible adventure and we have loved every minute. Every so often we take a step back to appreciate what the business has achieved. We are incredibly grateful for the experience and excited for the future.

We are thrilled to be able to share our knowledge and day-to-day experiences of the LOLA's baking world with you through our recipe book. This book is filled with 65 of our handpicked recipes, a few of LOLA's top secrets, a sprinkling of tips and a topping of helpful hints.

We hope that it inspires you to make cupcakes with LOLA and that each beautiful cupcake brings you as much joy as it has brought us.

BAKING & DECORATING TIPS

Your two main ingredients: be passionate about what you do and make your creations with love. Whatever happens along the way doesn't matter: the final product will be a result of the love and passion you put into your work.

We use muffin cases (38 mm/1½ inches across the base and 50 mm/2 inches high) for our regular cupcakes, and mini cases (22 mm/⅞ inch across the base and 31 mm/ 1¼ inches high) for our 'tinies'.

Decorate in a way you feel comfortable with; for example. At LOLA's we are all different but our cakes are always beautiful! Get creative and use different colours of frosting, bright sprinkles and edible glitter to make your cakes the centre of attention.

At LOLA's we mostly use large (18-mm/ ¾-inch) star shaped nozzles/tips, especially for our retail cupcakes, to get that perfect swirl. There are lots of sizes and shapes to choose from.

Remember sticky fingers make messy work, so always work as cleanly and neatly as possible. Imagine the mess we could make: in one day alone we can use more than 200 kg/441 lbs sugar, 24 litres/21 quarts milk and 40 kg/88 lbs butter and that's just to make the frosting!

When spreading frosting on cupcakes, a small spatula and a bowl of hot water are your best friends! Dipping the spatula in hot water will help you smooth your frosting beautifully. Be careful not to use too much water when smoothing, otherwise your frosting will split and crack.

There are lots of frostings to try in this book. We have teamed our favourites with the most perfect cupcake bases, but feel free to mix and match frostings. The same applies to toppings and decorations. The photos show how we like to serve our cupcakes, but the world is your oyster. Go on, give it a go!

LIGHTER SIDE OF DECADENCE

OFTEN KNOWN AS LIQUID GOLD, OLIVE OIL IS AN ENDLESS SOURCE OF FASCINATION IN OUR KITCHEN. IT MAKES THESE CUPCAKES DENSE AND RICH AND ADDS A HINT OF FRUITY FLAVOUR. THE FRESH PEARS PROVIDE THE PERFECT DOSE OF VITAMIN C AND A TOUCH OF SWEETNESS. THIS RECIPE IS ONE OF LOLA'S LITTLE TREASURES.

PEAR & OLIVE OIL

3 tablespoons sultanas/
  golden raisins
3 dessert pears
170 g/1⅓ cups plain/
  all-purpose flour
¼ teaspoon ground
  cinnamon
¾ teaspoon baking powder
¾ teaspoon bicarbonate
  of/baking soda
a pinch of salt
150 ml/⅔ cup olive oil
150 g/¾ cup (caster)
  sugar
grated zest of 1 lemon
½ vanilla pod/bean
2 large eggs, beaten
2 tablespoons apple juice
1 large egg white

MAPLE FROSTING
65 g/4 tablespoons butter,
  cubed and soft
3 tablespoons pure maple
  syrup, plus extra to drizzle
65 g/⅓ cup light
  muscovado sugar
150 g/5 oz. cream cheese,
  at room temperature

muffin pan lined with
  12 muffin cases

MAKES 12

Put the sultanas/golden raisins and 2 tablespoons water in a small saucepan and simmer over low heat until all the water has been absorbed. Remove from heat and let cool.

Preheat the oven to 180°C/350°F/ Gas 4.

Peel and grate 2 of the pears. Reserve the last pear for decorating.

Sift together the flour, ground cinnamon, baking powder, bicarbonate of/baking soda and salt in a bowl.

Put the olive oil and sugar in separate mixing bowl and beat with an electric hand mixer until combined. Add the lemon zest. Using a small, sharp knife, slit the vanilla pod/bean down its length and scrape the seeds out into the bowl containing the oil mixture. Gradually pour in the beaten eggs, whisking with the hand mixer until well combined. Mix in the grated pear and sultanas/golden raisins.

Now fold in the apple juice and sifted dry ingredients.

In a separate, grease-free bowl, whisk the egg white until soft peaks form. Gently fold into the cake mixture, being careful not to knock any air out.

Divide the mixture between the muffin cases. Bake in the preheated oven for 20–23 minutes or until well risen and a skewer inserted in the middle comes out clean. Remove from the oven and let cool completely on a wire rack before decorating.

MAPLE FROSTING
While the cupcakes are cooling down, make the maple frosting.

Put the butter, maple syrup and sugar in a bowl and beat with an electric hand mixer until light and creamy. Add the cream cheese and beat just until the frosting is very smooth.

Spread the frosting over the cold cupcakes using a spatula. Core the reserved pear and cut into thin wedges. Arrange on the cupcakes and drizzle with maple syrup.

GRANOLA IS A GREAT SOURCE OF DIETARY FIBRE, MAKING THIS CAKE THE PERFECT LOLA'S BREAKFAST SNACK. THE CUPCAKES SHOULD BE MADE WITH THE BEST CRUNCHY, NUTTY GRANOLA YOU CAN FIND. THEY ARE TOPPED WITH YOGURT FROSTING FOR A LOVELY FRESH FINISH.

GRANOLA & YOGURT

75 g/5 tablespoons butter, soft
140 g/¾ cup granulated sugar
1 large egg, beaten
2 teaspoons vanilla extract
300 g/1¼ cups fat-free plain yogurt
200 g/1½ cups plain/all-purpose flour
1 teaspoon bicarbonate of/baking soda
1 teaspoon baking powder
125 g/1 scant cup good-quality granola, plus extra to decorate

YOGURT FROSTING
130 g/½ cup Greek yogurt
1 teaspoon vanilla extract
350 g/2½ cups icing/confectioners' sugar

muffin pan lined with 12 muffin cases

MAKES 12

Preheat the oven to 180°C/350°F/Gas 4.

Put the butter and sugar in a mixing bowl and cream with an electric hand mixer. Stop occasionally to scrape down the side of the bowl with a rubber spatula. Add the beaten egg and beat until the mixture is light and fluffy.

Add the vanilla extract and yogurt. Beat on low speed until smooth, stopping once to scrape down the side of the bowl.

In a separate bowl, sift together the flour, bicarbonate of/baking soda and baking powder. Stir in the granola.

Add the dry ingredients to the egg mixture and stir until well mixed.

Divide the mixture between the muffin cases. Bake in the preheated oven for 18–20 minutes or until well risen and a skewer inserted in the middle comes out clean. Remove from the oven and let cool completely on a wire rack before decorating.

YOGURT FROSTING
While the cupcakes are cooling down, make the cream cheese frosting.

Put the Greek yogurt in a bowl and stir in the vanilla. Add one quarter of the icing/confectioners' sugar and stir until well combined. Repeat until all the sugar has been used up and you have a soft frosting.

Refrigerate for at least 45 minutes, or until firm enough to pipe.

Spread the frosting over the cold cupcakes using a spatula. Coat the cupcakes with granola, pressing it gently to the frosting to make it stick.

LOLA'S PRODUCT DEVELOPER TERRI WORKED TIRELESSLY TO HELP CREATE OUR BOOK. ORIGINALLY FROM NEW ZEALAND, SHE KNOWS ALL ABOUT MANUKA HONEY, WHICH IS GATHERED FROM BEES FEEDING ON MANUKA TREES IN THE EAST CAPE REGION. THE HONEY IS THOUGHT TO HAVE MAGICAL HEALING POWERS, SO GIVE THESE CUPCAKES A TRY!

MANUKA HONEY

175 g/¾ cup manuka honey, plus extra to top
100 ml/⅓ cup double/heavy cream
150 g/1 generous cup plain/all-purpose flour
1 teaspoon ground cinnamon
½ teaspoon ground mixed spice/apple pie spice
½ teaspoon baking powder
½ teaspoon bicarbonate of/baking soda
100 ml/½ cup sunflower oil
100 g/½ cup (caster) sugar
grated zest of ½ orange
¼ teaspoon instant coffee
2 large eggs
crushed honeycomb/sponge candy, to decorate

CREAM CHEESE FROSTING
50 g/3 tablespoons butter, cubed and soft
85 g/2½ oz. cream cheese
½ teaspoon vanilla extract
200 g/1½ cups icing/confectioners' sugar

muffin pan lined with 12 muffin cases

MAKES 12

Preheat the oven to 180°C/350°F/Gas 4.

Put the honey and cream in a saucepan and heat gently until melted and well mixed. Do not allow to come to a boil.

Meanwhile, sift together the flour, cinnamon, mixed spice/apple pie spice, baking powder and bicarbonate of/baking soda in a bowl.

Put the oil, sugar, orange zest and coffee granules in a mixing bowl and beat with an electric hand mixer until well mixed. Add the eggs, one at a time, beating well after each addition.

Fold in the sifted dry ingredients.

Finally, add the honey mixture and stir until well mixed.

Divide the mixture between the muffin cases. Bake in the preheated oven for 23–25 minutes or until well risen and a skewer inserted in the middle comes out clean. Remove from the oven and let cool completely on a wire rack before decorating.

CREAM CHEESE FROSTING
While the cupcakes are cooling down, make the cream cheese frosting.

Put the butter in a bowl and beat with an electric hand mixer until very soft and smooth. Add the cream cheese and vanilla and beat just to combine. Gradually sift the icing/confectioners' sugar into the bowl, beating until incorporated and the frosting is smooth and glossy.

Spread the frosting over the cold cupcakes using a spatula, or spoon the frosting into a piping bag fitted with a star nozzle/tip and pipe it on top of the cupcakes. Top with crushed honeycomb/sponge candy and a drizzle of manuka honey, if you like.

THIS IS WHAT WE CALL A GROWN-UP CAKE AT LOLA'S! IT IS LIGHT AND SIMPLE – HEAVENLY AT TEATIME. THE GINGER MAKES IT SPICY BUT NOT OVERPOWERING AND THE SLIGHT SHARPNESS OF THE FRESH LEMON BUTTERCREAM FROSTING COMPLEMENTS THE CAKE PERFECTLY.

GINGER LEMON

150 g/⅔ cup golden syrup or light corn syrup
170 ml/⅔ cup double/heavy cream
300 g/2⅓ cups plain/all-purpose flour
1 teaspoon ground cinnamon
1 tablespoon ground ginger
½ teaspoon ground cloves
2 teaspoons baking powder
¼ teaspoon bicarbonate of/baking soda
¼ teaspoon salt
125 g/1 stick butter, cubed and soft
180 g/1 scant cup packed dark brown sugar
3 eggs
crystallized ginger, to top

LEMON BUTTERCREAM
125 g/1 stick butter, cubed and soft
½ teaspoon vanilla extract
300 g/2¼ cups icing/confectioners' sugar
about 1 tablespoon milk
grated zest of 1 lemon, plus extra to decorate

muffin pan lined with 12 muffin cases

MAKES 12

Preheat the oven to 180°C/350°F/Gas 4.

Put the golden syrup or corn syrup and cream in a saucepan and heat gently until melted and well mixed. Do not allow to come to a boil.

Meanwhile, sift together the flour, ground cinnamon, ginger, cloves, baking powder, bicarbonate of/baking soda and salt in a bowl.

Put the butter and sugar in a mixing bowl and cream with an electric hand mixer until pale and fluffy. Stop occasionally to scrape down the side of the bowl with a rubber spatula. Add the eggs, one at a time, beating well after each addition.

Gradually add the syrup mixture and sifted dry ingredients alternately, beating well between each addition.

Divide the mixture between the muffin cases. Bake in the preheated oven for 20–23 minutes or until well risen and a skewer inserted in the middle comes out clean. Remove from the oven and let cool completely on a wire rack before decorating.

LEMON BUTTERCREAM
While the cupcakes are cooling down, make the lemon buttercream.

Put the butter in a bowl and beat with an electric hand mixer until very soft and smooth. Stir in the vanilla. Sift the icing/confectioners' sugar into the bowl in 4 batches, beating each batch until incorporated and the frosting is smooth. Add a little milk, if necessary, to loosen. Stir in the lemon zest.

Spread the frosting over the cold cupcakes using a spatula. Decorate with more zest and crystallized ginger.

EVERYONE DESERVES THE TASTE SENSATION THAT IS LOLA'S FAMOUS RED VELVET CUPCAKE. THEREFORE, BY POPULAR DEMAND FROM OUR CUSTOMERS, WE HAVE CREATED THE VEGAN RED VELVET, AND YOU WON'T KNOW THE DIFFERENCE! SEE PAGE 125 FOR OUR REGULAR RED VELVET, AS WELL AS A GLUTEN-FREE VERSION.

VEGAN RED VELVET

240 ml/1 cup plain soya milk
1 teaspoon apple cider vinegar
220 g/1¾ cups plain/ all-purpose flour
2 tablespoons cocoa powder
1 teaspoon baking powder
a pinch of salt
200 g/1 cup (caster) sugar
160 ml/⅔ cup vegetable oil
2 tablespoons red food colouring
2 teaspoons vanilla extract

VEGAN 'BUTTERCREAM'
200 g/1 cup soya spread/ natural (soy) buttery spread
1 tablespoon vanilla extract
750 g/5½ cups icing/ confectioners' sugar (see Notes opposite)
about 2–3 tablespoons soya milk

muffin pan lined with 12 muffin cases

MAKES 12

Preheat the oven to 190°C/375°F/ Gas 5.

Mix the soya milk and vinegar together in a bowl and set aside.

Sift the flour, cocoa powder, baking powder and salt in a mixing bowl. Add the sugar.

Add the oil, food colouring and vanilla to the soya-milk mixture and mix. Pour into the dry ingredients and mix. Transfer the cake mixture to a jug/ pitcher as it will be quite runny.

Pour the mixture evenly into the muffin cases. Bake in the preheated oven for about 20 minutes or until a skewer inserted in the middle comes out clean. Remove from the oven and let cool completely on a wire rack before decorating.

VEGAN 'BUTTERCREAM'
While the cupcakes are cooling down, make the vegan 'buttercream'.

Put the soya spread/natural buttery spread and vanilla in a mixing bowl.

Sift in the sugar. Beat with an electric hand mixer on slow speed until combined, then turn up the speed to medium–high and beat for 2–3 minutes. Add a little milk, if necessary, to loosen.

Slice a sliver of cake off the top of each cupcake with a sharp knife. Crumble it between your fingertips to make fine crumbs and set aside.

Spread the frosting over the cold cupcakes using a spatula, or spoon the frosting into a piping bag fitted with a star nozzle/tip and pipe it on top of the cupcakes. Top with the reserved red velvet crumbs.

NOTES
• Most icing/confectioners' sugar is vegan, but check the packaging before you buy. If in doubt, look for organic icing/confectioners' sugar, which tends to be vegan-friendly.
• Vegan-friendly ingredients are available at most health-food stores or major supermarkets.

WE CREATED THIS CUPCAKE ESPECIALLY FOR MOTHER'S DAY AT LOLA'S. IT IS AN INDULGENT TREAT BAKED WITH LEMON ZEST, COCONUT AND GROUND ALMONDS TO MAKE A SOFT, MOIST CAKE. TOPPED WITH A DOME OF LIGHT, WHIPPED LEMON MASCARPONE FROSTING AND FINISHED WITH DESICCATED COCONUT, THIS TROPICAL DELIGHT GOES DOWN WELL WITH MOTHERS EVERYWHERE!

LEMON COCONUT

70 g/½ cup plus
  1 tablespoon plain/
  all-purpose flour
1 teaspoon baking powder
a pinch of salt
200 g/1 stick plus
  5 tablespoons butter,
  cubed and soft
200 g/1 cup (caster) sugar
1 teaspoon vanilla extract
grated zest of ½ lemon
3 eggs
150 g/1 generous cup
  desiccated coconut,
  plus extra to decorate
70 g/½ cup ground
  almonds

LEMON MASCARPONE
FROSTING
240 ml/1 cup double/
  heavy cream
240 g/1 cup mascarpone
200 g/1½ cups icing/
  confectioners' sugar
grated zest of 1 lemon

*muffin pan lined with
  12 muffin cases*

MAKES 12

Preheat the oven to 180°C/350°F/ Gas 4.

Sift together the flour, baking powder and salt in a bowl.

Put the butter, sugar and vanilla in a mixing bowl and beat with an electric hand mixer until pale and fluffy. Stop occasionally to scrape down the side of the bowl with a rubber spatula. Add the lemon zest. Add the eggs, one at a time, beating well after each addition.

Add the sifted dry ingredients, desiccated coconut and almonds and beat on low speed until combined.

Divide the mixture between the muffin cases. Bake in the preheated oven for 20–25 minutes or until well risen and a skewer inserted in the middle comes out clean. Remove from the oven and let cool completely on a wire rack before decorating.

LEMON MASCARPONE FROSTING
While the cupcakes are cooling down, make the lemon mascarpone frosting.

Put the double/heavy cream in a bowl and whisk with an electric hand mixer on medium speed until soft peaks form – don't overwhisk, otherwise the cream will split or become grainy.

Put the mascarpone, sugar and lemon zest in a separate bowl and whisk with an electric hand mixer until smooth.

Fold the whipped cream gently into the mascarpone mixture.

Spread the frosting over the cold cupcakes using a spatula, making it into a neat dome shape. Pour desiccated coconut into a saucer and roll the tops of the cupcakes in the coconut to completely coat.

KAYLA FROM *VOGUE* MAGAZINE IS OUR SUPERFOOD GURU. SHE CREATED THIS EXOTIC, FRUITY CUPCAKE RECIPE WITH ALL THE BENEFITS OF THE ACAI BERRY. THE ACAI PALM TREE IS CULTIVATED FOR ITS FRUIT, WHICH LOOKS ALMOST LIKE A GRAPE BUT IS DEEP PURPLE IN COLOUR. IT IS SAID TO BE FILLED WITH ANTIOXIDANTS AND IS USED FREQUENTLY IN SUPERFOOD SMOOTHIES!

ACAI BERRY SUPERFOOD

250 g/2 cups self-rising
   flour
1 teaspoon baking powder
a pinch of salt
125 g/1 stick butter, cubed
   and soft
200 g/1 cup (caster) sugar
2 teaspoons lemon juice
grated zest of ½ lemon
3 eggs
100 ml/⅓ cup single/
   light cream
140 g/5 oz. açai berry
   pulp
blueberries, to decorate
edible glitter, to dust

ACAI BERRY CREAM
CHEESE FROSTING
80 g/5½ tablespoons
   butter, cubed and soft
360 g/2⅔ cups icing/
   confectioners' sugar
150 g/5 oz. cream cheese
30 g açai berry pulp

*muffin pan lined with
12 muffin cases*

MAKES 12

Preheat the oven to 180°C/350°F/
Gas 4.

   Sift together the flour, baking powder and salt in a bowl.

   Put the butter and sugar in a mixing bowl and beat with an electric hand mixer until pale and fluffy. Stop occasionally to scrape down the side of the bowl with a rubber spatula. Add the lemon juice and zest. Add the eggs, one at a time, beating well after each addition.

   Pour in one third of the sifted dry ingredients and beat on low speed. Add half the cream and beat well. Repeat this process, then finish with the last third of the dry ingredients. Finally, fold in the açai berry pulp.

   Divide the mixture between the muffin cases. Bake in the preheated oven for 20–25 minutes or until well risen and a skewer inserted in the middle comes out clean. Remove from the oven and let cool completely on a wire rack before decorating.

ACAI BERRY CREAM CHEESE
FROSTING
While the cupcakes are cooling down, make the açai berry cream cheese frosting.

   Put the butter in a bowl and beat with an electric hand mixer on high speed until until pale and fluffy, about 2–3 minutes. Gradually sift in the sugar and beat until well mixed. Stop occasionally to scrape down the side of the bowl with a rubber spatula. Add the cream cheese and beat in. Finally, gently fold in the açai berry pulp until combined. Don't worry if the frosting looks runny – refrigerate for at least 1 hour, until firm enough to pipe.

   Spread the frosting over the cold cupcakes using a spatula, or spoon the frosting into a piping bag fitted with a star nozzle/tip and pipe it on top of the cupcakes. Top with blueberries and dust with edible glitter.

NOTE
Açai powder, capsules and drinks are available from healthfood stores. The pulp is available online, or blueberries can be substituted.

LOLA'S MANGO BERRY SWIRL WAS CREATED TO CELEBRATE SUMMER AND OUR FAVOURITE FRUIT, MANGOES. WE RECOMMEND USING THE FRESHEST, RIPEST, FINELY CHOPPED MANGOES TO GET THE BEST FLAVOUR AND TEXTURE IN THE CUPCAKE – AS WELL AS A GOOD DOSE OF VITAMIN C. OUR SEASONAL MIXED BERRY MASCARPONE FROSTING ON TOP MAKES THIS A REALLY FRUITY TASTE SENSATION!

MANGO BERRY SWIRL

125 g/1 cup self-rising flour
1 teaspoon baking powder
125 g/¾ cup ground almonds
75 g/6 tablespoons butter, cubed and soft
125 g/⅔ cup (caster) sugar
grated zest of ½ lemon
2 eggs
70 g/⅓ cup crème fraîche
100 g/⅔ cup finely chopped fresh mango
mixed berries, to decorate

BERRY MASCARPONE FROSTING
110 g/1 scant cup blueberries
90 g/¾ cup raspberries
100 g/1 scant cup strawberries
200 g/1 cup (caster) sugar
600 g/2½ cups mascarpone

muffin pan lined with 12 muffin cases

MAKES 12

Preheat the oven to 180°C/350°F/Gas 4.

Sift together the flour and baking powder in a bowl. Stir in the almonds.

Put the butter and sugar in a mixing bowl and beat with an electric hand mixer until pale and fluffy. Stop occasionally to scrape down the side of the bowl with a rubber spatula. Add the lemon zest. Add the eggs, one at a time, beating well after each addition.

Add the dry ingredients and crème fraîche and beat on low speed until combined. Fold in the chopped mango.

Divide the mixture between the muffin cases. Bake in the preheated oven for 20–25 minutes or until well risen and a skewer inserted in the middle comes out clean. Remove from the oven and let cool completely on a wire rack before decorating.

BERRY MASCARPONE FROSTING
While the cupcakes are cooling down, make the berry mascarpone frosting.

Put all the berries and the sugar in a saucepan over medium heat. Bring to a simmer and let simmer for about 25–35 minutes until thickened. Remove from the heat and let cool.

Put the cooled berry mixture in a food processor or blender and blitz to a purée.

Add the purée to the mascarpone in batches and mix gently until fully incorporated. Refrigerate for at least 30 minutes, or until firm enough to pipe.

Spread the frosting over the cold cupcakes using a spatula, or spoon the frosting into a piping bag fitted with a star nozzle/tip and pipe it on top of the cupcakes. Top with mixed berries.

THIS WAS CREATED TO SPICE UP ANY HALLOWEEN OR THANKSGIVING PARTY! IT IS A VERY MOIST CAKE, FULL OF AROMATIC SPICES, AND TOPPED WITH A HEAVENLY CINNAMON CREAM CHEESE FROSTING.

PUMPKIN CINNAMON

75 g/⅔ cup shelled
   pecans, plus 12 to top
190 g/1½ cups plain/
   all-purpose flour
1½ teaspoons ground
   cinnamon, plus extra
   to dust
¾ teaspoon ground nutmeg
1½ teaspoons baking
   powder
¾ teaspoon bicarbonate
   of/baking soda
a pinch of salt
100 g/6½ tablespoons
   butter, cubed and soft
60 g/¼ cup plus
   2 tablespoons dark
   brown sugar
60 g/¼ cup (caster) sugar
½ vanilla pod/bean
2 eggs
175 g/¾ cup canned
   pumpkin purée
60 ml/¼ cup sour cream

CINNAMON CREAM CHEESE FROSTING
140 g/9½ tablespoons
   butter, cubed and soft
225 g/1⅔ cups icing/
   confectioners' sugar
210 g/1 scant cup cream
   cheese
2 teaspoons ground
   cinnamon
1½ teaspoons vanilla extract

*muffin pan lined with
   12 muffin cases*

MAKES 12

Preheat the oven to 180°C/350°F/ Gas 4.

To toast the pecans, set a frying pan over medium–high heat to warm up. Add the pecans to the warm pan and toast, stirring frequently, for about 5–8 minutes. Remove from the heat and let cool slightly.

Put the cooled, toasted pecans in a food processor and grind to a powder. Set aside.

Sift together the flour, ground cinnamon, nutmeg, baking powder, bicarbonate of/baking soda and salt in a bowl.

Put the butter and sugars in a mixing bowl and cream with an electric hand mixer until light and fluffy. Stop occasionally to scrape down the side of the bowl with a rubber spatula.

Using a small, sharp knife, slit the vanilla pod/bean down its length and scrape the seeds out into the mixing bowl. Add the eggs, one at a time, beating well after each addition.

Add the sifted dry ingredients and beat on low speed until combined.

Finally, fold in the pumpkin purée, sour cream and ground pecans.

Divide the mixture between the muffin cases. Bake in the preheated oven for 25–30 minutes or until well risen and a skewer inserted in the middle comes out clean. Remove from the oven and let cool completely on a wire rack before decorating.

CINNAMON CREAM CHEESE FROSTING
While the cupcakes are cooling down, make the cinnamon cream cheese frosting.

Put the butter in a bowl and beat with an electric hand mixer on high speed until until pale and fluffy, about 2–3 minutes. Sift in the sugar and beat on medium speed for 3–5 minutes until well mixed. Stop occasionally to scrape down the side of the bowl with a rubber spatula. Finally, add the cream cheese, ground cinnamon and vanilla and beat until fluffy.

Spread the frosting over the cold cupcakes using a spatula, or spoon the frosting into a piping bag fitted with a large, plain nozzle/tip and pipe it on top of the cupcakes. Top with a pecan and dust with ground cinnamon.

THIS IS LOLA'S TAKE ON THE AMERICAN CLASSIC BLUEBERRY MUFFIN. THESE CUPCAKES ARE LIGHT, MOIST AND BURSTING WITH ANTIOXIDANT-FILLED BLUEBERRIES. THEY'RE TOPPED WITH A LUXURIOUSLY CREAMY WHITE CHOCOLATE FROSTING THAT COMBINES BEAUTIFULLY WITH BLUEBERRIES! AS ONE OF OUR SUMMER SEASONAL BESTSELLERS, THIS IS DEFINITELY A MUST-TRY TREAT.

BLUEBERRY WHITE CHOCOLATE

150 g/1¼ cups self-rising flour
1½ teaspoons baking powder
90 g/⅔ cup ground almonds
120 g/1 stick butter, cubed and soft
180 g/¾ cup plus 2 tablespoons (caster) sugar
a few drops vanilla extract
grated zest of ½ lemon
2 eggs
90 ml/⅓ cup plus 1 tablespoon plain yogurt
120 g/1¼ cups blueberries, plus extra to decorate
blueberry jam, to drizzle

WHITE CHOCOLATE FROSTING
50 ml/3 tablespoons double/heavy cream
140 g/4½ oz. white chocolate, finely chopped
300 g/1¼ cups mascarpone
3 tablespoons icing/ confectioners' sugar

muffin pan lined with 12 muffin cases

MAKES 12

Preheat the oven to 180°C/350°F/ Gas 4.

Sift together the flour and baking powder in a bowl. Stir in the almonds.

Put the butter, sugar and vanilla in a mixing bowl and beat with an electric hand mixer until pale and fluffy. Stop occasionally to scrape down the side of the bowl with a rubber spatula. Add the lemon zest. Add the eggs, one at a time, beating well after each addition.

Add the dry ingredients and yogurt and beat on low speed until combined. Fold in the blueberries.

Divide the mixture between the muffin cases. Bake in the preheated oven for 20–25 minutes or until well risen and a skewer inserted in the middle comes out clean. Remove from the oven and let cool completely on a wire rack before decorating.

WHITE CHOCOLATE FROSTING
While the cupcakes are cooling down, make the white chocolate frosting.

Put the cream in a saucepan over medium heat and heat until just starting to bubble around the edges. Remove from the heat and stir in the chocolate. Stir until the chocolate has melted and you have a glossy ganache. Let cool for a few minutes.

Put the mascarpone and sugar in a mixing bowl and beat with an electric hand mixer until soft peaks form.

Gently fold the melted chocolate into the whipped mascarpone. Refrigerate for 1–2 hours, or until firm enough to pipe.

Spread the frosting over the cold cupcakes using a spatula, or spoon the frosting into a piping bag fitted with a star nozzle/tip and pipe it on top of the cupcakes.

Put the blueberry jam in a small saucepan and heat gently for about 30 seconds or until slightly runny.

Top the cupcakes with a cluster blueberries and a drizzle of the runny blueberry jam.

THIS IS LOLA'S TAKE ON THE WORLD-RENOWNED SOUTHERN GERMAN DESSERT, *SCHWARZWÄLDER KIRSCHTORTE*, OTHERWISE KNOWN AS BLACK FOREST CAKE. INDULGE YOURSELF IN THIS HEAVENLY, MOIST AND RICHLY CHOCOLATEY CAKE WITH A HINT OF SWEETNESS FROM THE CHERRY JAM MIXED INTO THE CUPCAKE BATTER. FOR AN EXTRA KICK, ADD A DASH OF SCHWARZWÄLDER KIRSCH, THE SPECIALTY GERMAN BRANDY WITH ITS DISTINCTIVE CHERRY-PIT FLAVOUR.

CHERRY CHOCOLATE

125 g/1 stick butter
100 g/3½ oz. dark/ bittersweet chocolate, finely chopped
300 g/1¼ cups cherry jam
150 g/¾ cup (caster) sugar
a pinch of salt
2 eggs, lightly beaten
150 g/1 cup plus 3 tablespoons self-rising flour
chocolate curls, to decorate
12 cherries

DARK CHOCOLATE GANACHE
100 g/3½ oz. dark/ bittersweet chocolate, finely chopped
100 ml/scant ½ cup double/heavy cream
150 g/1 generous cup icing/confectioners' sugar

muffin pan lined with 12 muffin cases

MAKES 12

Preheat the oven to 180°C/350°F/ Gas 4.

Put the butter in a large saucepan over low heat and allow to melt. Once the butter is nearly completely melted, stir in the chocolate and let soften for 1 minute. Now remove the pan from the heat and stir the mixture with a wooden spoon until thoroughly melted and smooth. Add the cherry jam, sugar, salt and eggs. Stir until well mixed.

Finally, fold in the flour.

Divide the mixture between the muffin cases. Bake in the preheated oven for about 25 minutes or until well risen and a skewer inserted in the middle comes out clean. Remove from the oven and let cool completely on a wire rack before decorating.

DARK CHOCOLATE GANACHE
While the cupcakes are cooling down, make the dark chocolate ganache.

Put the chocolate and cream in a saucepan over low heat. Heat gently until the chocolate starts to melt, whisking occasionally with a balloon whisk. Continue until the chocolate has melted and the ganache is thick and smooth. Sift the sugar into the pan and whisk until the ganache is smooth.

Transfer the ganache to a bowl and refrigerate for 30–40 minutes, or until firm. Spread it over the cold cupcakes using a spatula.

Pour some chocolate curls into a saucer and roll the edge of each cupcake in the curls to coat. Top with a perfect cherry.

LOLA'S CREATED THIS CUPCAKE TO RAISE MONEY FOR THE JAPANESE RED CROSS SOCIETY FOLLOWING THE DEVASTATING TSUNAMI ON 11 MARCH 2010. CHERRY BLOSSOM TREES ARE A SYMBOL OF FRIENDSHIP IN JAPAN, SO WE THOUGHT THIS CUPCAKE WOULD BE THE PERFECT WAY TO SHOW OUR SUPPORT. THE ALMONDS AND CHERRIES MARRY REALLY WELL TOGETHER, BEING, IN FACT, CLOSE BOTANICAL RELATIVES.

VANILLA CHERRY BLOSSOM

100 g/¾ cup self-rising flour
70 g/½ cup plain/
   all-purpose flour
¾ teaspoon baking powder
a pinch of salt
95 g/6½ tablespoons
   butter, cubed and soft
150 g/¾ cup (caster) sugar
¼ teaspoon vanilla extract
2 eggs
85 ml/⅓ cup whole milk
90 g/⅓ cup Morello cherry
   jam
2 tablespoons toasted
   flaked/slivered almonds
12 edible pink flowers
edible glitter, to dust

CHERRY BLOSSOM
FROSTING
75 g/⅓ cup Morello cherry
   jam
125 g/1 stick butter, cubed
   and soft
1 teaspoon vanilla extract
500 g/3⅔ cups icing/
   confectioners' sugar
about 1 tablespoon milk

*muffin pan lined with
   12 muffin cases*

MAKES 12

Preheat the oven to 190°C/375°F/ Gas 5.

Sift together the flours, baking powder and salt in a bowl.

Put the butter, sugar and vanilla in a mixing bowl and beat with an electric hand mixer until pale and fluffy. Stop occasionally to scrape down the side of the bowl with a rubber spatula. Add the eggs, one at a time, beating well after each addition.

Add the sifted dry ingredients and milk alternately and beat on low speed until combined.

Put the cherry jam in a small saucepan and heat gently for about 30 seconds or until slightly runny. Pour the warm, runny jam into the cake mixture and roughly swirl it in. Don't mix it in too much.

Divide the mixture between the muffin cases, making sure they are no more than three quarters full. Sprinkle the toasted almonds on top of the cupcakes and press down gently into the mixture.

Bake in the preheated oven for about 20 minutes or until well risen and a skewer inserted in the middle comes out clean. Remove from the oven and let cool completely on a wire rack before decorating.

CHERRY BLOSSOM FROSTING

While the cupcakes are cooling down, make the cherry blossom frosting.

Put the cherry jam in a small saucepan and heat gently for about 30 seconds or until slightly runny. Strain the warm jam and discard any bits. Set aside the smooth jam to cool slightly.

Put the butter in a bowl and beat with an electric hand mixer until very soft and smooth. Stir in the vanilla. Sift half the icing/confectioners' sugar into the bowl, beating until incorporated and the frosting is smooth. Add the second half of the sugar, as well as the smooth jam, and beat for 5 minutes until thick and creamy. Add a little milk, if necessary, to loosen.

Spread the frosting over the cold cupcakes using a spatula, or spoon the frosting into a piping bag fitted with a large, plain nozzle/tip and pipe it on top of the cupcakes. Top with an edible pink flower and a sprinkle of glitter.

THIS IS LOLA'S TAKE ON LEMON MERINGUE PIE. IT'S A DELICATE LEMON
CUPCAKE TOPPED WITH MERINGUE AND HIDDEN INSIDE IS A POOL
OF PASSIONFRUIT CURD, IN HONOUR OF OUR SOUTH AFRICAN ROOTS.
PIPE THE MERINGUE IN LITTLE PEAKS FOR A VERY IMPRESSIVE FINISH!

PASSIONFRUIT MERINGUE

PASSIONFRUIT CURD
3 eggs
1 egg yolk
100 ml/scant ½ cup
   passionfruit juice (from
   about 6 fruits), sifted and
   pips reserved (optional)
175 g/¾ cup plus 2
   tablespoons (caster) sugar
125 g/1 stick butter, cubed

CUPCAKE MIXTURE
125 g/1 cup self-rising
   flour
1 teaspoon baking powder
75 g/½ cup ground
   almonds
100 g/6½ tablespoons
   butter, cubed and soft
150 g/¾ cup (caster) sugar
½ teaspoon vanilla extract
grated zest of ½ lemon
2 eggs
75 ml/⅓ cup plain yogurt

MERINGUE TOPPING
3 egg whites
180 g/1 cup caster/
   superfine sugar
¼ teaspoon cream of tartar
½ teaspoon vanilla extract

*muffin pan lined with
   12 muffin cases
sugar thermometer
kitchen blowtorch*

MAKES 12

PASSIONFRUIT CURD
Start by making the passionfruit curd.
   Mix the whole eggs and egg yolk
together in a heatproof bowl.
   Put the passionfruit juice and sugar
in a saucepan and bring to a boil. Boil
until the sugar has dissolved. Slowly
pour the hot fruit syrup into the eggs,
stirring briskly and constantly to prevent
the eggs from scrambling.
   Bring a small saucepan of water to
a gentle simmer and set the bowl of egg
mixture on the pan. Heat, stirring gently,
for 20–30 minutes or until thick enough
to coat the back of a wooden spoon.
Remove from the heat and whisk in the
butter, a few pieces at a time. Let cool
and refrigerate for at least 4 hours, or
overnight if possible.

CUPCAKE MIXTURE
Preheat the oven to 180°C/350°F/
Gas 4.
   Sift together the flour and baking
powder in a bowl. Stir in the almonds.
   Put the butter, sugar and vanilla in
a mixing bowl and beat with an electric
hand mixer until pale and fluffy. Stop
occasionally to scrape down the side
of the bowl with a rubber spatula. Add
the lemon zest. Add the eggs, one at
a time, beating well after each addition.
   Add the dry ingredients and yogurt
and beat on low speed until combined.
   Divide the mixture between the

muffin cases. Bake in the preheated
oven for 20–25 minutes or until well
risen and a skewer inserted in the
middle comes out clean. Remove from
the oven and let cool completely on
a wire rack before decorating.

MERINGUE TOPPING
Mix the egg whites, sugar and cream of
tartar in a heatproof bowl. Bring a small
saucepan of water to a gentle simmer
and set the bowl of egg whites on the
pan. Heat, whisking with a balloon
whisk, until the sugar has dissolved and
a sugar thermometer in the mixture reads
60°C/140°F.
   Remove from the heat and whisk
with an electric hand mixer on low
speed and gradually increasing to high
speed. Whisk until stiff, glossy (but not
dry) peaks have formed. Whisk in the
vanilla. Refrigerate for 10–15 minutes
or until firm enough to pipe.
   When the cupcakes are completely
cold, make a hole in the middle with a
teaspoon and fill with a dollop of curd.
Spread the meringue over the cold
cupcakes using a spatula, or spoon the
meringue into a piping bag fitted with
a star nozzle/tip and pipe it in little
peaks on top of the cupcakes.
   Hold a kitchen blowtorch about
10 cm/4 inches from the meringue and
scorch evenly. Pour passionfruit pips on
top, if desired.

THIS RECIPE PAYS TRIBUTE TO OUR FAVOURITE BRITISH JAM, MARMALADE, TRADITIONALLY MADE FROM THE JUICE AND PEEL OF ORANGES. ADDING IT TO THE CAKE MIXTURE KEEPS THE CAKE MOIST, AND THE BUTTERCREAM IS ENRICHED WITH MORE MARMALADE AND MARSHMALLOW FLUFF (OR MELTED MINI MARSHMALLOWS IF YOU PREFER).

MARMALADE MALLOW

1 egg
3 egg whites
250 g/1¼ cups (caster) sugar
185 g/1½ sticks butter, cubed and soft
½ teaspoon baking powder
¼ teaspoon salt
255 g/2 cups plain/ all-purpose flour
½ teaspoon ground cinnamon
½ teaspoon ground nutmeg
a pinch of ground cloves
¼ teaspoon vanilla extract
120 ml/½ cup milk
100 g/about ⅓ cup orange marmalade
grated orange zest, to top

MARMALADE MALLOW BUTTERCREAM
90 g/⅓ cup orange marmalade
250 g/2 sticks butter, soft
40 g/½ cup Marshmallow Fluff (see Note opposite)
½ teaspoon vanilla extract
400 g/3 cups icing/ confectioners' sugar
about 1 tablespoon milk

muffin pan lined with 12 muffin cases

MAKES 12

Preheat the oven to 180°C/350°F/ Gas 4.

Put the egg and egg whites, sugar and butter in a mixing bowl and beat with an electric hand mixer.

Add all the remaining ingredients except the marmalade and beat until just combined.

Put the marmalade in a small saucepan and heat gently for about 30 seconds or until slightly runny. Chop up any large bits of orange peel.

Spoon a little of the cupcake mixture into each muffin case, just to cover the bottom. Spoon about ½ teaspoon of the warm marmalade into each muffin case on top of the mixture.

Divide the remaining mixture between the muffin cases. Bake in the preheated oven for about 25 minutes or until well risen and a skewer inserted in the middle comes out clean. Remove from the oven and let cool completely on a wire rack before decorating.

MARMALADE MALLOW BUTTERCREAM

While the cupcakes are cooling down, make the marmalade mallow buttercream.

Chop up any large bits of orange peel in the marmalade.

Put the butter, Marshmallow Fluff, marmalade and vanilla in a mixing bowl and beat with an electric hand mixer until creamy. Gradually sift in the sugar and mix in. Add a little milk, if necessary, to loosen.

Spread the frosting over the cold cupcakes using a spatula, or spoon the frosting into a piping bag fitted with a star nozzle/tip and pipe it on top of the cupcakes. Top with grated orange zest.

NOTE
In the UK, Marshmallow Fluff is becoming more widely available. You can find in larger supermarkets, gourmet food stores and online through Amazon and www.americanfooduk.co.uk

LOLA'S GLUTEN-FREE ORANGE CHOCOLATE CUPCAKE IS A CHARMING FLAVOUR COMBINATION INSPIRED BY A POPULAR BRITISH TREAT CALLED A CHOCOLATE ORANGE. WE ARE A LITTLE OBSESSED BY CITRUS IN OUR BAKERY, SO IT WAS EASY TO CREATE THIS MOUTHWATERING CUPCAKE, BURSTING WITH FRESH ORANGE. OUR HEAVENLY CHOCOLATE GANACHE-STYLE FROSTING FINISHES THIS OFF PERFECTLY. TO ADD TO THE BENEFITS OF THIS CUPCAKE (AS IF WE NEEDED TO!), IT'S GLUTEN FREE, SO THOSE WHO ARE GLUTEN-INTOLERANT NEEDN'T MISS OUT.

GLUTEN-FREE ORANGE CHOCOLATE

2 whole oranges, scrubbed but not peeled, and thinly sliced
600 g/3 cups (caster) sugar
4 eggs
200 g/1½ cups ground almonds
1 teaspoon baking powder
candied orange peel or grated orange zest, to top

DARK CHOCOLATE FROSTING
100 ml/⅓ cup double/ heavy cream
150 g/5 oz. dark/ bittersweet chocolate, finely chopped
600 g/2½ cups mascarpone cheese

muffin pan lined with 12 muffin cases

MAKES 12

Put the sliced oranges, 500 g/2½ cups of the sugar and 250 ml/1 cup water in a saucepan and bring to a boil. Reduce the heat to low and simmer, uncovered, for 1½ hours, or until the liquid has almost evaporated and the oranges are coated in syrup.

Transfer the contents of the pan to a blender or food processor and blitz until smooth. Let cool. This purée can be prepared a day in advance and refrigerated until needed.

Preheat the oven to 180°C/350°F/ Gas 4.

Put the eggs and remaining sugar in a mixing bowl and whisk with an electric hand mixer until just combined. Add the almonds and baking powder and whisk again. Add the orange purée and whisk until well mixed.

Divide the mixture between the muffin cases. Bake in the preheated oven for 25–30 minutes or until they spring back when you press them, and a skewer inserted in the middle comes out clean. They will not rise very much. Remove from the oven and let cool completely on a wire rack before decorating.

DARK CHOCOLATE FROSTING
Put the cream in a saucepan over medium heat and heat until just starting to bubble around the edges.

Remove from the heat and stir in the chocolate. Stir until the chocolate has melted and you have a glossy ganache. Let cool for a few minutes.

Fold in the mascarpone and mix gently until evenly incorporated. Spread the frosting over the cold cupcakes using a spatula. Decorate with candied orange peel or grated orange zest.

BISCOTTI ARE A TWICE-BAKED ITALIAN COOKIE. DELICATELY FLAVOURED, CRISP AND CRUMBLY, THEY SEEM TO CALL OUT TO BE TEAMED WITH A RECIPE LIKE THIS: A DENSE, CARAMEL-SWEET CUPCAKE FINISHED WITH AN UTTERLY IRRESISTIBLE, STICKY-SWEET CARAMEL CHOCOLATE GANACHE. IF YOU HAVE SOME GANACHE LEFT OVER, DUNK A SPARE BISCOTTI IN IT FOR AN EXTRA-INDULGENT TREAT!

CARAMEL BISCOTTI

150 g/1⅓ cups plain/
  all-purpose flour
50 g/⅓ cup self-rising flour
125 g/1 stick butter, cubed
  and soft
150 g/¾ cup dark brown
  sugar
90 g/3 oz. white
  chocolate, melted
90 g/⅓ cup golden syrup
  or light corn syrup
1 egg
½ teaspoon vanilla extract
125 ml/½ cup milk
12 small biscotti, to top

CARAMEL CHOCOLATE GANACHE

100 g/½ cup (caster) sugar
¾ teaspoon lemon juice
225 ml/1 cup pouring or
  whipping cream
300 g/10 oz. milk
  chocolate, finely chopped

*muffin pan lined with
  12 muffin cases*

MAKES 12

Preheat the oven to 180°C/350°F/Gas 4.

Sift together the flours in a bowl.

Put the butter and sugar in a mixing bowl and beat with an electric hand mixer until pale and fluffy. Stop occasionally to scrape down the side of the bowl with a rubber spatula.

Add the melted chocolate and golden or corn syrup and mix until smooth. Add the egg and vanilla, beating on slow speed until well mixed.

Add the sifted flours and milk in alternate batches, gently folding them in. Do not overmix and be as gentle and brief as possible.

Divide the mixture between the muffin cases. Bake in the preheated oven for 20–25 minutes or until well risen and a skewer inserted in the middle comes out clean. Remove from the oven and let cool completely on a wire rack before decorating.

CARAMEL CHOCOLATE GANACHE

While the cupcakes are cooling down, make the caramel chocolate ganache.

Put the sugar, lemon juice and 60 ml/¼ cup water in a saucepan and stir. Cook over medium–high heat until the sugar dissolves, then cook without stirring until dark caramel in colour, about 7–10 minutes.

Remove the pan from the heat, add the cream and stir briskly to combine – beware that the sugar syrup will be dangerously hot and will bubble and spit when you pour the cream in.

Add the chocolate and stir until melted and smooth. Let cool completely, whisking occasionally (about 1 hour). Refrigerate for 1–2 hours or until firm enough to pipe, whisking occasionally.

Spread the ganache over the cold cupcakes using a spatula. Top with a small biscotti.

LOOKING FOR AN ALTERNATIVE TO THE PEANUT BUTTER AND JELLY SANDWICH? LOLA'S HAS THE ANSWER. OUR TRIBUTE CUPCAKE IS BASED ON A NUTTY CAKE CONCEALING A TREASURE OF STRAWBERRY JELLY/JAM. THE PRETTY BUT DECADENT PEANUT AND JELLY FROSTING PACKS A SWEET PUNCH. WE REALLY LOVE THIS CUPCAKE.

PEANUT BUTTER & JELLY

200 g/1⅔ cups plain/
   all-purpose flour
1½ teaspoons baking
   powder
175 g/1½ sticks butter,
   cubed and soft
200 g/1 cup packed dark
   brown sugar
1 teaspoon vanilla extract
200 g/¾ cup smooth
   all-natural peanut butter
2 large eggs
150 ml/⅔ cup milk
170 g/¾ cup strawberry
   jam/jelly

PEANUT BUTTER & JELLY
FROSTING
70 g/½ cup finely chopped
   unsalted roasted peanuts,
   plus extra to decorate
2 teaspoons vegetable oil
120 g/1 stick butter, cubed
   and soft
1 teaspoon vanilla extract
500 g/3⅔ cups icing/
   confectioners' sugar
2 tablespoons strawberry
   jam/jelly, plus extra to top
1–2 tablespoons milk

*muffin pan lined with
   12 muffin cases*

MAKES 12

Preheat the oven to 180°C/350°F/Gas 4.

Sift together the flour and baking powder in a bowl.

Put the butter, sugar and vanilla in a mixing bowl and beat with an electric hand mixer until pale and fluffy. Stop occasionally to scrape down the side of the bowl with a rubber spatula. Add the peanut butter and beat again. Add the eggs, one at a time, beating well after each addition.

Fold in the sifted dry ingredients and milk alternately.

Divide just half the mixture between the muffin cases. Drop a teaspoon of jam into each cupcake case, then divide the remaining cupcake mixture between the cases.

Bake in the preheated oven for 20–25 minutes or until well risen and a skewer inserted in the middle comes out clean (except for a smudge of jam!). Remove from the oven and let cool completely on a wire rack before decorating.

PEANUT BUTTER & JELLY FROSTING

While the cupcakes are cooling down, make the peanut butter & jelly frosting.

Put the peanuts and oil in a food processor and blitz until smooth.

Put the butter in a bowl and beat with an electric hand mixer until very soft and smooth. Stir in the vanilla. Sift in half the sugar, beating until blended. Add the second half of the sugar and beat on low speed. Add the jam and peanut paste and beat again. Slowly pour in the milk and when it is mixed in, beat for 3–5 minutes on a higher speed.

Put some extra jam, for drizzling, in a small saucepan and heat gently for about 30 seconds or until slightly runny. Strain the warm jam and discard any bits. Let cool slightly.

Spread the frosting over the cold cupcakes using a spatula, or spoon the frosting into a piping bag fitted with a star nozzle/tip and pipe it on top of the cupcakes. Drizzle the runny jam on top and scatter chopped peanuts over it.

SINCE ELVIS HAD NEARLY AS MANY FANS AS LOLA'S, WE NAMED A
CUPCAKE AFTER HIS FAVOURITE SANDWICH – FRIED PEANUT BUTTER
AND BANANAS. OUR DEDICATION COMBINES THE GOOD, THE BAD
AND THE YUMMY. LOLA'S HR GURU, NICKY, IS A HUGE ELVIS FAN,
SO THIS ONE IS ESPECIALLY FOR HER!

ELVIS

190 g/1½ cups plus
   1 tablespoon plain/
   all-purpose flour
½ teaspoon ground
   cinnamon
¼ teaspoon ground nutmeg
1 teaspoon baking powder
¾ teaspoon bicarbonate
   of/baking soda
a pinch of salt
125 g/1 stick butter, cubed
   and soft
60 g/⅓ cup packed dark
   brown sugar
60 g/¼ cup (caster) sugar
½ vanilla pod/bean
2 eggs
2 ripe bananas, mashed
75 g/⅔ cup chopped
   unsalted roasted peanuts,
   plus extra to decorate

PEANUT BUTTERCREAM
200 g/1⅔ sticks butter,
   cubed and soft
400 g/3 cups icing/
   confectioners' sugar
3 tablespoons milk
115 g/½ cup smooth
   all-natural peanut butter

*muffin pan lined with
   12 muffin cases*

MAKES 12

Preheat the oven to 180°C/350°F/
Gas 4.

Sift together the flour, ground
cinnamon, nutmeg, baking powder,
bicarbonate of/baking soda and salt
in a bowl.

Put the butter and sugars in a mixing
bowl and beat with an electric hand
mixer until pale and fluffy. Stop
occasionally to scrape down the side
of the bowl with a rubber spatula.

Using a small, sharp knife, slit the
vanilla pod/bean down its length and
scrape the seeds out into the mixing
bowl. Add the eggs, one at a time,
beating well after each addition.

Slowly add the sifted dry ingredients
and beat on low speed until combined.
Fold in the mashed banana and
chopped peanuts.

Divide the mixture between the
muffin cases. Bake in the preheated

oven for 25–30 minutes or until well
risen and a skewer inserted in the
middle comes out clean. Remove from
the oven and let cool completely on
a wire rack before decorating.

PEANUT BUTTERCREAM
While the cupcakes are cooling down,
make the peanut buttercream.

Put the butter in a bowl and beat
with an electric hand mixer until very
soft and smooth. Sift half the sugar into
the bowl, beating until incorporated
and the frosting is smooth.

Add the second half of the sugar,
as well as the milk, and beat for
3–5 minutes until thick and creamy.
Finally, fold in the peanut butter.

Spread the frosting over the cold
cupcakes using a spatula. Decorate
with chopped peanuts.

LOLA'S HI-HAT MARSHMALLOW CUPCAKES ARE REAL FUN TO MAKE AND EAT! A SCRUMPTIOUS DARK CHOCOLATE CUPCAKE IN COMBINATION WITH A THICK SWISS MERINGUE AND A CRUNCHY CHOCOLATE SHELL GIVE THESE THE WOW FACTOR FOR ANY OCCASION.

HI-HAT MARSHMALLOW

100 g/3½ oz. dark/
   bittersweet chocolate
   (70% cocoa), chopped
175 g/1 stick plus
   5 tablespoons butter
225 g/1 cup plus
   2 tablespoons (caster)
   sugar
4 eggs
100 g/¾ cup self-rising
   flour
3 tablespoons cocoa
   powder
a pinch of salt

EASY MARSHMALLOW
FROSTING
180 g/1 scant cup (caster)
   sugar
¼ teaspoon cream of tartar
3 egg whites
½ teaspoon vanilla extract

CHOCOLATE COATING
350 g/12 oz. good-quality
   milk chocolate, chopped
3 tablespoons vegetable oil

muffin pan lined with
   12 muffin cases

MAKES 12

Preheat the oven to 180°C/350°F/Gas 4.

Put the chocolate and butter in a heatproof bowl over a pan of simmering water. Do not let the base of the bowl touch the water. Heat, stirring, until the chocolate melts and you have a smooth, glossy mixture. Remove from the heat and stir in the sugar. Let cool for 10 minutes.

Now beat with an electric hand mixer for 3 minutes. Add the eggs, one at a time, beating for 10 seconds between each addition. Sift the flour, cocoa and salt into the bowl and beat until blended.

Divide the mixture between the muffin cases. Bake in the preheated oven for 20–25 minutes or until well risen and a skewer inserted in the middle comes out clean. Remove from the oven and let cool completely on a wire rack before decorating.

EASY MARSHMALLOW FROSTING

While the cupcakes are cooling down, make the easy marshmallow frosting.

Whisk the sugar, cream of tartar, egg whites and 60 ml/¼ cup water in a large heatproof bowl with an electric hand mixer on high speed until foamy, about 1 minute. Bring a small saucepan

of water to a gentle simmer and set the bowl on the pan. Beat on high speed until stiff peaks form, about 5 minutes. Remove from the heat, stir in the vanilla and beat for a further 2 minutes, or until the frosting is nice and thick.

Transfer the frosting to a piping bag fitted with a plain 1-cm/⅜-inch nozzle/tip. Leaving a narrow border around the very edge, pipe a spiral of frosting about 5 cm/2 inches high around each cold cupcake.

Set aside while you prepare the chocolate coating.

CHOCOLATE COATING

Put the chocolate and oil in a heatproof bowl over a pan of simmering water. Do not let the base of the bowl touch the water. Heat, stirring, until the chocolate melts and you have a glossy mixture.

Transfer to a small, deep bowl and let cool for 15 minutes.

Holding each cupcake by the base, dip the marshmallow spiral into the cooled, melted chocolate to entirely coat the spiral. You shouldn't be able to see any of the marshmallow, so fill in any gaps with a little more chocolate. Allow the excess to drip off.

Let the cupcakes stand on a wire rack to set at room temperature for 15 minutes before serving.

S'MORES

120 g/4 oz. digestive
   biscuits/graham crackers
   (about 8 altogether),
   crushed, plus extra to
   decorate
2½ tablespoons butter,
   melted
150 g/1 cup plus
   3 tablespoons plain/
   all-purpose flour
1 teaspoon baking powder
a pinch of salt
180 g/1 stick plus
   5 tablespoons butter,
   cubed and soft
150 g/¾ cup packed light
   brown sugar
1 teaspoon vanilla extract
2 eggs, at room
   temperature
150 ml/⅔ cup milk
12 squares of milk
   chocolate
dark chocolate, melted,
   to decorate

MARSHMALLOW
FROSTING
180 g/1 scant cup (caster)
   sugar
¼ teaspoon cream of tartar
3 egg whites
1 teaspoon vanilla extract

muffin pan lined with
*   12 muffin cases*
sugar thermometer

MAKES 12

Preheat the oven to 180°C/350°F/
Gas 4.

Mix three quarters of the crushed
digestive biscuits/graham crackers with
the melted butter. Place 1 teaspoon of
this into each muffin case – enough
to cover the base of the case.

Sift together the flour, baking
powder and salt in a bowl. Add the
remaining biscuit/cracker crumbs and
mix well.

Put the cubed butter, sugar and
vanilla in a mixing bowl and beat with
an electric hand mixer until pale and
fluffy. Stop occasionally to scrape
down the side of the bowl with a rubber
spatula. Add the eggs, one at a time,
beating well after each addition.

Pour in one third of the dry
ingredients and beat on low speed.
Add half the milk and beat well.
Repeat this process, then finish with
the last third of the dry ingredients.

Divide the mixture between the
muffin cases. Bake in the preheated
oven for 25–30 minutes or until well
risen and a skewer inserted in the
middle comes out clean. Remove from
the oven and let cool completely on
a wire rack before decorating.

MARSHMALLOW
FROSTING
While the cupcakes are
cooling down, make the
marshmallow frosting.

Put the sugar, cream of tartar
and 100 ml/⅓ cup water in a
saucepan and mix well. Heat until
the sugar has dissolved and a
sugar thermometer in the mixture
reads 115°C/242°F.

Meanwhile, in a separate, grease-
free heatproof bowl, whisk the egg
whites with an electric hand mixer until
stiff peaks form. Pour a thin, slow stream
of the sugar syrup into the egg whites,
whisking constantly, until the frosting
stands in peaks. Make sure the syrup
goes straight into the egg whites and
doesn't hit the beaters otherwise sugar
crystals will form. Stir in the vanilla.
Refrigerate for 30 minutes, or until firm
enough to pipe.

Spread the frosting over the cold
cupcakes using a spatula, or spoon the
frosting into a piping bag fitted with a
star nozzle/tip and pipe it on top of the
cupcakes. Pour some crushed biscuits/
crackers into a saucer and roll the edge
of each cupcake in the crumbs to coat.
Top with a square of milk chocolate and
drizzle with melted chocolate.

A S'MORE TRADITIONALLY CONSISTS OF A ROASTED MARSHMALLOW
AND A LAYER OF CHOCOLATE SANDWICHED BETWEEN TWO COOKIES.
MEET LOLA'S S'MORES CUPCAKE: A REAL FEEL-GOOD INDULGENCE!

LOLA'S CREATED THIS CUPCAKE TO CELEBRATE BRITISH FOOD FORTNIGHT AT HARRODS. THIS ALMOST-TOO-GOOD-TO-BE-TRUE CUPCAKE IS ULTRA STICKY AND SWEET. IT'S NOT ONLY TOPPED WITH BUTTERSCOTCH, BUT FILLED WITH A WHISKY-FUELLED BUTTERSCOTCH FOR AN EXTRA KICK.

BUTTERSCOTCH PIE

175 g/1⅓ cups plain/
  all-purpose flour
1 teaspoon baking powder
a pinch of salt
150 g/1¼ sticks butter,
  cubed and soft
150 g/¾ cup (caster)
  sugar
½ vanilla pod/bean
3 eggs
12 or 24 cubes of fudge

BUTTERSCOTCH FILLING
100 g/½ cup (caster) sugar
2 tablespoons butter
50 ml/3 tablespoons
  double/heavy cream
2 teaspoons whisky

BUTTERSCOTCH ICING
100 g/6½ tablespoons
  butter
200 g/1 cup packed dark
  brown sugar
175 ml/⅔ cup double/
  heavy cream
1 teaspoon black treacle/
  dark molasses
½ teaspoon vanilla extract
a pinch of salt

*muffin pan lined with
  12 muffin cases or mini-
  cupcake pan lined with
  24 mini-cupcake cases*

MAKES 12 REGULAR
OR 24 TINY

Preheat the oven to 180°C/350°F/Gas 4.

Sift together the flour, baking powder and salt in a bowl.

Put the butter and sugar in a mixing bowl and beat with an electric hand mixer until pale and fluffy. Stop occasionally to scrape down the side of the bowl with a rubber spatula. Using a small, sharp knife, slit the vanilla pod/bean down its length and scrape the seeds out into the mixing bowl. Add the eggs, one at a time, beating well after each addition.

Slowly add the sifted dry ingredients and beat on low speed until combined.

Divide the mixture between the muffin cases. Bake in the preheated oven for 20–25 minutes for regular cupcakes, or a little less for tiny cupcakes. They should well risen and a skewer inserted in the middle should come out clean. Remove from the oven and let cool completely on a wire rack while you make the butterscotch filling for the inside of the cupcakes.

BUTTERSCOTCH FILLING

Scatter the sugar evenly over the base of a heavy-based saucepan and set over medium heat. Do not stir. When it has melted and starts to turn an amber colour, remove from the heat and add the butter. Add the cream and whisky and whisk thoroughly with a balloon whisk until well mixed. Let cool.

BUTTERSCOTCH ICING

While the filling is cooling down, make the butterscotch icing.

Melt the butter in a heavy-based saucepan. Add the sugar and mix. Cook over medium heat for about 4–5 minutes, stirring occasionally. Add 125 ml/½ cup of the cream and whisk to mix. Cook for 8–10 minutes, stirring occasionally with a balloon whisk. It will bubble and froth as it's cooking. Remove from the heat and let cool for 20 minutes, then stir in the remaining cream, the treacle/molasses, vanilla and salt. Let cool to room temperature.

When the cupcakes are completely cold, make a hole in the middle by scooping out a neat portion of the cake with a teaspoon. Fill the hole with a dollop of the reserved butterscotch filling. Put the portion of cake back on top of the filling.

Spread a thin layer of butterscotch icing onto the cold cupcakes with a spatula. Top with a cube of fudge.

LOLA'S CHOCOLATE MARSHMALLOW CUPCAKE IS AS RICH, DARK AND DANGEROUS AS IT'S UTTERLY IRRESISTIBLE. IT HAS MINI MARSHMALLOWS MIXED INTO A CHOCOLATE CUPCAKE, MARSHMALLOW FROSTING AND MORE MINI MARSHMALLOWS ON TOP. IN THE UK, THIS COMBINATION OF FLAVOURS IS FOUND IN TEACAKES, BUT ONE OF THESE CUPCAKES MAKES AN EVEN BETTER ACCOMPANIMENT TO COFFEE OR TEA.

CHOCOLATE MARSHMALLOW

140 g/1 cup plus
   2 tablespoons plain/
   all-purpose flour
30 g/¼ cup cocoa powder
1 teaspoon baking powder
90 g/6 tablespoons butter,
   cubed and soft
170 g/¾ cup (caster) sugar
½ teaspoon vanilla extract
2 eggs
125 ml/½ cup milk
35 g/generous ½ cup mini
   marshmallows, plus extra
   to decorate
storebought chocolate
   sauce, to drizzle

MARSHMALLOW
FROSTING
180 g/1 scant cup (caster)
   sugar
¼ teaspoon cream of tartar
3 egg whites
1 teaspoon vanilla extract

muffin pan lined with
   12 muffin cases
sugar thermometer

MAKES 12

Preheat the oven to 180°C/350°F/ Gas 4.

Sift together the flour, cocoa powder and baking powder in a bowl.

Put the butter, sugar and vanilla in a mixing bowl and beat with an electric hand mixer until pale and fluffy. Stop occasionally to scrape down the side of the bowl with a rubber spatula. Add the eggs, one at a time, beating well after each addition.

Add the sifted dry ingredients and milk in alternate batches and beat on low speed until combined. Fold in the mini marshmallows.

Divide the mixture between the muffin cases. Bake in the preheated oven for about 25 minutes or until well risen and a skewer inserted in the middle comes out clean. Remove from the oven and let cool completely on a wire rack before decorating.

MARSHMALLOW FROSTING
While the cupcakes are cooling down, make the marshmallow frosting.

Put the sugar, cream of tartar and 100 ml/⅓ cup water in a saucepan and mix well. Heat until the sugar has dissolved and a sugar thermometer in the mixture reads 115°C/242°F.

Meanwhile, in a separate, grease-free heatproof bowl, whisk the egg whites with an electric hand mixer until stiff peaks form. Pour a thin, slow stream of the sugar syrup into the egg whites, whisking constantly, until the frosting stands in peaks. Make sure the syrup goes straight into the egg whites and doesn't hit the beaters otherwise sugar crystals will form. Stir in the vanilla. Refrigerate for 30 minutes.

Spread the frosting over the cold cupcakes using a spatula. Top with mini marshmallows and chocolate sauce.

IT GOES WITHOUT SAYING THAT IF YOU'RE A COOKIE DOUGH FAN,
THESE CUPCAKES ARE PERFECT FOR YOU! FROM THE CHOCOLATE CHIP-
STUDDED CAKE TO THE SCRUMPTIOUS COOKIE-DOUGH FILLING TO THE
BROWN-SUGAR COOKIE FROSTING, THIS CUPCAKE IS UTTERLY YUMMY.
WE HAVE LEFT OUT THE RAW EGG YOU WOULD NORMALLY FIND IN
RAW COOKIE DOUGH AND IT IS AS GOOD, IF NOT BETTER, WITHOUT.

COOKIE DOUGH

COOKIE DOUGH
2 tablespoons butter, soft
50 g/¼ cup packed light
   brown sugar
75 g/⅔ cup plain/
   all-purpose flour
3 tablespoons sweetened
   condensed milk
¼ teaspoon vanilla extract
3 tablespoons milk
   chocolate chips

CUPCAKE MIXTURE
200 g/1⅔ cups plain/
   all-purpose flour
½ teaspoon baking powder

½ teaspoon bicarbonate
  of/baking soda
¼ teaspoon salt
180 g/1½ sticks butter,
  cubed and soft
175 g/¾ cup packed light
  brown sugar
1 teaspoon vanilla extract
2 eggs
2½ tablespoons milk
60 g/½ cup milk chocolate
  chips

COOKIE FROSTING
175 g/1½ sticks butter,
  cubed and soft
150 g/¾ cup packed light
  brown sugar
150 g/1 generous cup
  icing/confectioners' sugar
50 g/⅓ cup plain/
  all-purpose flour
a pinch of salt
3 tablespoons milk
1 teaspoon vanilla extract
12 chocolate chip cookies

*muffin pan lined with
  12 muffin cases*

MAKES 12

COOKIE DOUGH

To make the cookie dough, cream
the butter and sugar in a bowl with an
electric hand mixer on medium–high
speed until light and fluffy, about
2 minutes. Beat in the flour, condensed
milk and vanilla until smooth. Stir in the
chocolate chips. Cover and refrigerate
until firmer, about 1 hour.

CUPCAKE MIXTURE

Preheat the oven to 180°C/350°F/
Gas 4.

Sift together the flour, baking
powder, bicarbonate of/baking soda
and salt in a bowl.

Put the butter, sugar and vanilla in
a mixing bowl and beat with an electric
hand mixer until pale and fluffy. Stop
occasionally to scrape down the side
of the bowl with a rubber spatula. Add
the eggs, one at a time, beating well
after each addition.

Pour in one third of the sifted dry
ingredients and beat on low speed.
Add half the milk and beat well.

Repeat this process, then finish with
the last third of the dry ingredients.
Fold in the chocolate chips.

Divide the mixture between the
muffin cases. Bake in the preheated
oven for 18–20 minutes or until well
risen and a skewer inserted in the
middle comes out clean. Remove from
the oven and let cool completely on
a wire rack before decorating.

When the cupcakes are completely
cold, make a hole in the middle with
a teaspoon and fill with a chunk of the
chilled cookie dough.

COOKIE FROSTING

While the cupcakes are cooling down,
make the cookie frosting.

Cream the butter and brown sugar
together in a bowl with an electric hand
mixer. Mix in the icing/confectioners'
sugar until smooth. Beat in the flour and
salt. Finally, beat in the milk and vanilla
until smooth.

Spread the frosting over the cold
cupcakes using a spatula, or spoon the
frosting into a piping bag fitted with
a star nozzle/tip and pipe it on top
of the cupcakes. Top with a cookie.

THIS IS THE ULTIMATE IN DECADENCE. AN UNBELIEVABLY MOIST CAKE
MADE WITH DEEP, DARK CHOCOLATE CONTAINING AT LEAST 70%
COCOA SOLIDS, IT IS ENRICHED WITH DARK CHOCOLATE GANACHE
AND TOPPED WITH THE SAME. FOR AN EXTRA INDULGENCE, FINISH
WITH A RICH AND ELEGANT TRUFFLE COATED IN COCOA POWDER.
SO DECADENT, SO DELICIOUS AND SO PERFECT.

DARK CHOCOLATE TRUFFLE

DARK CHOCOLATE GANACHE

225 ml/1 cup double/
   heavy cream
175 g/6 oz. dark/
   bittersweet chocolate
   (70% cocoa), finely
   chopped
1 teaspoon vanilla extract
a pinch of salt

CUPCAKE MIXTURE

100 g/3½ oz. dark/
   bittersweet chocolate
   (70% cocoa), chopped
175 g/1½ sticks butter
225 g/1 cup plus 2
   tablespoons (caster)
   sugar
4 eggs
100 g/¾ cup self-rising
   flour
2 tablespoons cocoa
   powder
a pinch of salt
12 truffles

*muffin pan lined with
   12 muffin cases*

MAKES 12

DARK CHOCOLATE GANACHE

Start by making the dark chocolate ganache.

Put the cream in a saucepan over medium heat and heat until just starting to bubble around the edges.

Remove from the heat and stir in the chocolate. Stir until the chocolate has melted and you have a glossy ganache. Stir in the vanilla and salt. Let cool and firm up while you make the cupcakes.

CUPCAKE MIXTURE

Preheat the oven to 180°C/350°F/ Gas 4.

Put the chocolate and butter in a heatproof bowl over a pan of simmering water. Do not let the base of the bowl touch the water. Heat, stirring, until the chocolate melts and you have a smooth, glossy mixture. Remove from the heat and stir in the sugar. Let cool for about 10 minutes.

Now beat the slightly cooled chocolate mixture with an electric hand mixer for 3 minutes. Add the eggs, one at a time, beating for 10 seconds between each addition. Sift the flour, cocoa and salt into the bowl and beat until blended.

Take 4 tablespoons of the ganache and beat it briefly into the cupcake mixture until just combined.

Divide the mixture between the muffin cases. Bake in the preheated oven for 20–25 minutes or until well risen and a skewer inserted in the middle comes out clean. Remove from the oven and let cool completely on a wire rack before decorating.

While the cupcakes are baking and cooling, put the remaining chocolate ganache in the refrigerator to chill for 30–40 minutes.

Spread the remaining chocolate ganache over the cold cupcakes using a spatula. Top with a truffle.

THIS PRETTY TREAT DEFIES WHAT'S KNOWN AS THE 'PISTACHIO EFFECT'. THIS IS WHERE FOODS TASTE BETTER BECAUSE THEY REQUIRE SOME EFFORT BEFORE THEY CAN BE CONSUMED, LIKE REMOVING THE SHELLS FROM PISTACHIOS. MAKING THIS CUPCAKE REQUIRES LITTLE WORK, BUT IT TASTES SUBLIME! THE NUTS PROVIDE GREAT FLAVOUR AND COLOUR.

PISTACHIO CHOCOLATE CHIP

115 g/1 scant cup plain/
  all-purpose flour
1 teaspoon baking powder
a pinch of salt
100 g/6½ tablespoons
  butter, cubed and soft
170 g/¾ cup (caster) sugar
½ teaspoon vanilla extract
2 eggs
40 ml/3 tablespoons
  single/light cream
110 g/¾ cup shelled
  unsalted pistachios,
  ground
75 g/½ cup milk chocolate
  chips
finely chopped pistachios,
  to decorate

MILK CHOCOLATE MOUSSE FROSTING
125 ml/½ cup double/
  heavy cream
125 g/4 oz. milk
  chocolate, finely chopped
125 g/1 stick butter, cubed
  and soft
400 g/3 cups icing/
  confectioners' sugar
1 tablespoon cocoa powder

*muffin pan lined with
  12 muffin cases*

MAKES 12

Preheat the oven to 180°C/350°F/ Gas 4.

Sift together the flour, baking powder and salt in a bowl.

Put the butter, sugar and vanilla in a mixing bowl and beat with an electric hand mixer until pale and fluffy. Stop occasionally to scrape down the side of the bowl with a rubber spatula. Add the eggs, one at a time, beating well after each addition.

Add the sifted dry ingredients and cream in alternate batches and beat on low speed until combined. Fold in the ground pistachios and chocolate chips.

Divide the mixture between the muffin cases. Bake in the preheated oven for 25–30 minutes or until well risen and a skewer inserted in the middle comes out clean. Remove from the oven and let cool completely on a wire rack before decorating.

MILK CHOCOLATE MOUSSE FROSTING

While the cupcakes are cooling down, make the milk chocolate mousse frosting.

Put the cream in a saucepan over medium heat and heat until just starting to bubble around the edges.

Remove from the heat and stir in the chocolate. Stir until the chocolate has melted and you have a glossy ganache. Let cool to room temperature.

When the ganache is at room temperature, put the butter in a mixing bowl. Beat with an electric hand mixer until light and fluffy. Add the sugar, cocoa and ganache and beat on slow speed until combined, then increase the speed to medium and beat for 3 minutes, or until light. Refrigerate for 30 minutes, or until firm enough to pipe.

Spread the frosting over the cold cupcakes using a spatula, or spoon the frosting into a piping bag fitted with a star nozzle/tip and pipe it on top of the cupcakes. Top with chopped pistachios.

LOLA'S HAZELNUT PRALINE RECIPE MAKES A DELECTABLY CRUNCHY CUPCAKE THAT LOOKS SUPERB AND WILL GET YOUR TASTE BUDS BUZZING. IF YOU CAN'T GET ENOUGH OF THE PRALINE FLAVOUR, ADD A DASH OF NUT-FLAVOURED LIQUEUR LIKE FRANGELICO TO THE BUTTERCREAM FROSTING. FOR ADULTS ONLY!

HAZELNUT PRALINE

180 g/1⅓ cups plain/ all-purpose flour
1¼ teaspoons baking powder
¼ teaspoon salt
150 g/1¼ sticks butter, cubed and soft
150 g/¾ cup (caster) sugar
1 tablespoon hazelnut oil
45 g/⅓ cup blanched hazelnuts, finely chopped
2 eggs, beaten
150 ml/⅔ cup sour cream

HAZELNUT PRALINE
185 g/1½ cups blanched hazelnuts
125 g/⅔ cup (caster) sugar
1 tablespoon butter

HAZELNUT BUTTERCREAM
120 g/1 stick butter, cubed and soft
1 teaspoon vanilla extract
500 g/3⅔ cups icing/ confectioners' sugar
2–4 tablespoons milk

muffin pan lined with 12 muffin cases
baking sheet lined with non-stick parchment paper

MAKES 12

Preheat the oven to 170°C/325°F/ Gas 3.

Sift together the flour, baking powder and salt in a bowl.

Put the butter, sugar, oil and finely chopped hazelnuts in a mixing bowl and beat with an electric hand mixer until light and airy. Stop occasionally to scrape down the side of the bowl with a rubber spatula. Gradually add the eggs, beating well after each addition.

Fold in half the sifted dry ingredients then half the sour cream. Repeat with the remaining dry ingredients, then the cream.

Divide the mixture between the muffin cases. Bake in the preheated oven for 20–25 minutes or until well risen and a skewer inserted in the middle comes out clean. Remove from the oven and let cool completely on a wire rack before decorating. Leave the oven on.

HAZELNUT PRALINE
Put the hazelnuts on a baking sheet and roast in the hot oven for 5–10 minutes.

Meanwhile, scatter the sugar evenly over the base of a heavy-based saucepan and set over medium heat. Do not stir. When it has melted and starts to turn an amber colour, remove from the heat and add the butter and

just two thirds of the roasted hazelnuts and mix. (Reserve the remaining roasted nuts for the buttercream.) Pour onto the prepared, lined baking sheet.

As soon as the mixture has cooled down and set, roughly grind most of it in a food processor or finely chop with a sharp knife. Chop the remaining praline into chunks. Reserve both forms of praline for decorating.

HAZELNUT BUTTERCREAM
Grind the reserved roasted nuts in a food processor. They will eventually turn to a sticky paste.

Put the butter in a bowl and beat with an electric hand mixer until very soft and smooth. Stir in the vanilla. Sift half the icing/confectioners' sugar into the bowl, beating until incorporated. Add the second half of the sugar and beat on low speed. Slowly pour in the milk and, when it is mixed in, beat for 3–5 minutes on a higher speed.

Add the hazelnut paste and beat in.

Spread the frosting over the cold cupcakes using a spatula, or spoon the frosting into a piping bag fitted with a star nozzle/tip and pipe it on top of the cupcakes. Pour the reserved ground praline into a saucer and roll the edge of each cupcake in the pieces to coat. Top with some of the praline chunks.

LOLA'S FUDGE BROWNIE CUPCAKE WAS CREATED IN OUR KITCHENS TO CELEBRATE NATIONAL CHOCOLATE WEEK IN THE UK. IT IS DENSE AND RICH AND WONDERFULLY FUDGY. THE GOOEY CHOCOLATE GIVES IT WARMTH AND THE NUTS ADD A FABULOUS CRUNCH. WITH THE CUBE OF BROWNIE ON TOP, INDULGENT DOESN'T BEGIN TO DESCRIBE IT.

FUDGE BROWNIE

250 g/2 cups plain/
    all-purpose flour
1 teaspoon baking powder
a pinch of salt
190 g/6½ oz. dark/
    bittersweet chocolate
    (70% cocoa), chopped
130 g/1 stick butter, cubed
    and soft
250 g/1¼ cups caster or
    packed dark brown sugar
2 teaspoons vanilla extract
2 eggs
60 g/½ cup chopped nuts
    (optional)
60 g/2 oz. white chocolate,
    chopped (optional)
storebought milk chocolate
    sauce, to drizzle
12 cubes of brownie

CARAMEL CHOCOLATE GANACHE
100 g/½ cup (caster) sugar
¾ teaspoon lemon juice
225 ml/1 cup pouring or
    whipping cream
300 g/10 oz. milk
    chocolate, finely chopped

*muffin pan lined with
    12 muffin cases*

MAKES 12

Preheat the oven to 180°C/350°F/ Gas 4.

Sift together the flour, baking powder and salt in a bowl.

Put the chocolate and butter in a heatproof bowl over a pan of simmering water. Do not let the base of the bowl touch the water. Heat, stirring, until the chocolate melts and you have a smooth, glossy mixture. Remove from the heat and beat in the sugar and vanilla with an electric hand mixer.

Add the eggs, one at a time and beat briefly until just combined. Reduce the speed to low and add the sifted dry ingredients. Beat briefly again just until combined. Stir in the chopped nuts and white chocolate, if using.

Divide the mixture between the muffin cases. Bake in the preheated oven for 25–30 minutes or until well risen and a skewer inserted in the middle comes out clean. Remove from the oven and let cool completely on a wire rack before decorating.

CARAMEL CHOCOLATE GANACHE
While the cupcakes are cooling down, make the caramel chocolate ganache.

Put the sugar, lemon juice and 60 ml/¼ cup water in a saucepan and stir. Cook over medium–high heat until the sugar dissolves, then cook without stirring until dark caramel in colour, about 7–10 minutes.

Remove the pan from the heat, add the cream and stir briskly to combine – beware that the sugar syrup will be dangerously hot and will bubble and spit when you pour the cream in.

Add the chocolate and stir until melted and smooth. Let cool completely, whisking occasionally (about 1 hour). Refrigerate for 1–2 hours, whisking occasionally.

Spread the frosting over the cold cupcakes using a spatula. Drizzle with chocolate sauce and top with a cube of brownie.

HERE IS OUR VERSION OF THE POPULAR ICE CREAM DESSERT. MADE WITH THE SAME CUPCAKE BASE AS THE FUDGE BROWNIE RECIPE ON THE PREVIOUS PAGE, THIS IS AN ALTOGETHER SWEETER TREAT. LADEN WITH VANILLA ICE CREAM, CARAMEL SAUCE, CHERRIES AND WAFERS, IT TAKES SUNDAES TO NEW LEVELS! DESPITE ITS NAME, THIS IS DEFINITELY A RECIPE TO TRY ON ANY DAY OF THE WEEK!

CHOCOLATE SUNDAE

250 g/2 cups plain/
   all-purpose flour
1 teaspoon baking powder
a pinch of salt
190 g/6½ oz. dark/
   bittersweet chocolate
   (70% cocoa), chopped
130 g/1 stick butter, cubed
   and soft
250 g/1¼ cups caster or
   (packed) dark brown
   sugar
2 teaspoons vanilla extract
2 eggs
120 g/1 cup chopped nuts

CARAMEL SAUCE
75 g/5 tablespoons butter
75 g/⅓ cup packed dark
   brown sugar
100 ml/⅓ cup double/
   heavy cream

TO DECORATE
vanilla ice cream
12 cherries
12 wafer tubes

*muffin pan lined with
   12 muffin cases*

MAKES 12

Preheat the oven to 180°C/350°F/ Gas 4.

Sift together the flour, baking powder and salt in a bowl.

Put the chocolate and butter in a heatproof bowl over a pan of simmering water. Do not let the base of the bowl touch the water. Heat, stirring, until the chocolate melts and you have a smooth, glossy mixture. Remove from the heat and beat in the sugar and vanilla with an electric hand mixer.

Add the eggs, one at a time and beat briefly until just combined. Reduce the speed to low and add the sifted dry ingredients. Beat briefly again just until combined.

Stir in the chopped nuts.

Divide the mixture between the muffin cases. Bake in the preheated oven for 25–30 minutes or until well risen and a skewer inserted in the middle comes out clean. Remove from the oven and let cool completely on a wire rack before decorating.

CARAMEL SAUCE
To make the caramel sauce, put the butter and sugar in a small saucepan and cook over low heat until melted and smooth. Gradually add the cream. Let cool slightly before using.

TO DECORATE
Meanwhile, remove the ice cream from the freezer 15 minutes before you are ready to assemble the cupcakes.

Spoon the softened ice cream into a piping bag fitted with a star nozzle/tip and pipe it on top of the cupcakes. Top with a cherry and a wafer tube and drizzle with caramel sauce.

Serve and eat immediately, before the ice cream melts.

IN JAPAN, BENTO IS A SINGLE-PORTION MEAL, WHICH PERFECTLY DESCRIBES THIS CUPCAKE – TOO GOOD TO SHARE! A CHOCOLATEY CAKE STUDDED WITH CHUNKS OF MILK CHOCOLATE AND CONTAINING A MELTING CARAMEL AT ITS HEART, THEN DECORATED WITH UNCTUOUS WHITE CHOCOLATE CREAM CHEESE FROSTING. WE THINK THIS SWEET MEAL-IN-ONE IS TOTALLY WORTH IT!

MELTED BENTO

95 g/¾ cup self-rising flour
60 g/½ cup cocoa powder
a pinch of salt
125 g/1 stick butter, melted
225 g/1 cup plus 2
    tablespoons (caster) sugar
1 teaspoon vanilla extract
2 eggs, beaten
175 g/6 oz. milk
    chocolate, chopped
12 caramel-filled chocolates
chocolate sticks, to decorate

WHITE CHOCOLATE CREAM CHEESE FROSTING
50 ml/3 tablespoons
    double/heavy cream
150 g/5 oz. white
    chocolate, chopped
60 g/5 tablespoons butter,
    cubed and soft
250 g/1⅔ cups icing/
    confectioners' sugar
125 g/4 oz. cream cheese

*muffin pan lined with
    12 muffin cases*

MAKES 12

Preheat the oven to 180°C/350°F/Gas 4.

Sift together the flour, cocoa powder and salt in a bowl.

Put the melted butter, sugar, vanilla and beaten eggs in a mixing bowl and beat with an electric hand mixer until well mixed.

Mix in the sifted dry ingredients and chopped chocolate.

Divide just half the mixture between the muffin cases. Put a caramel-filled chocolate in each cupcake on top of the mixture, then divide the remaining mixture between the cases.

Bake in the preheated oven for 25–30 minutes or until well risen. Remove from the oven and let cool completely on a wire rack before decorating.

WHITE CHOCOLATE CREAM CHEESE FROSTING
While the cupcakes are cooling down, make the white chocolate cream cheese frosting.

Put the cream in a saucepan over medium heat and heat until just starting to bubble around the edges.

Remove from the heat and stir in the chocolate. Stir until the chocolate has melted and you have a glossy ganache. Let cool to room temperature.

When the ganache is at room temperature, put the butter in a mixing bowl. Beat with an electric hand mixer until light and fluffy. Add the sugar and cream cheese and beat for 2–3 minutes. Beat in the white chocolate ganache. Refrigerate for 1 hour, or until firm enough to pipe.

Spread the frosting over the cold cupcakes using a spatula, or spoon the frosting into a piping bag fitted with a star nozzle/tip and pipe it on top of the cupcakes. Decorate with chocolate sticks, broken into short lengths.

LOLA'S CARAMEL APPLE MUESLI CUPCAKE WAS INSPIRED BY TWO OF OUR FAVOURITE DESSERTS – THE TRADITIONAL BRITISH APPLE CRUMBLE AND AMERICAN CARAMEL APPLES. IN ADDITION TO THE CARAMEL CUPCAKE, WE HAVE A SMOOTH CARAMEL CREAM CHEESE FROSTING TOPPED WITH APPLE PUREE AND MUESLI, FOR A TOUCH OF CRUNCH.

CARAMEL APPLE MUESLI

2 small dessert apples
150 g/1⅓ cups plain/
   all-purpose flour
50 g/⅓ cup self-rising flour
125 g/1 stick butter, cubed
   and soft
150 g/¾ cup packed dark
   brown sugar
90 g/3 oz. white
   chocolate, melted
90 g/⅓ cup golden syrup
   or light corn syrup
1 egg
½ teaspoon vanilla extract
125 ml/½ cup milk
muesli, for sprinkling

CARAMEL CREAM CHEESE FROSTING
50 g/¼ cup granulated
   sugar
2½ tablespoons double/
   heavy cream
65 g/½ stick butter, cubed
   and soft
185 g/1⅓ cups icing/
   confectioners' sugar
250 g/8 oz. cream cheese

*muffin pan lined with
   12 muffin cases*

MAKES 12

Preheat the oven to 180°C/350°F/ Gas 4.

To make an apple purée, peel and core the apples, then roughly chop. Put the apple chunks and 3 tablespoons water in a small saucepan, cover and cook over low heat for 5–8 minutes or until very soft. Mash with a fork or potato masher until smooth. Let cool.

Meanwhile, sift together the flours in a bowl.

Put the butter and sugar in a mixing bowl and beat with an electric hand mixer until pale and fluffy. Stop occasionally to scrape down the side of the bowl with a rubber spatula. Add the melted chocolate and golden syrup or corn syrup and mix until smooth. Add the egg and vanilla and beat on slow speed for 30 seconds.

Slowly add the sifted flours and milk in alternate batches and beat until combined. Divide the mixture between the muffin cases. Bake in the preheated oven for 20–25 minutes or until well risen and a skewer inserted in the middle comes out clean. Remove from the oven and let cool completely on a wire rack before decorating.

CARAMEL CREAM CHEESE FROSTING

While the cupcakes are cooling down, make the caramel cream cheese frosting.

Put the sugar and 2 tablespoons water in a saucepan and stir. Bring to a boil over medium–high heat, then cook without stirring until dark amber in colour, about 7–10 minutes.

Remove the pan from the heat, add the cream and stir briskly to combine – beware that the sugar syrup will be dangerously hot and will bubble and spit when you pour the cream in. Let cool for 8–10 minutes or until cooler but still warm and pourable.

Put the butter in a mixing bowl. Beat with an electric hand mixer until light and fluffy. Add the icing/confectioners' sugar and cream cheese and beat for 2–3 minutes. Beat in the warm caramel. Refrigerate for 1 hour, or until firm enough to pipe.

Spread the frosting over the cold cupcakes using a spatula. Spread a strip of apple purée down the middle of the frosting and sprinkle some muesli directly on top.

THIS LOLA'S CUPCAKE WAS CREATED TO CELEBRATE THANKSGIVING AND THE AUTUMN MONTHS. OUR VERSION OF THE MUCH-LOVED PECAN PIE IS A LIGHT CAKE EMBELLISHED WITH A PECAN PIE FILLING.

PECAN PIE

200 g/1⅔ cups plain/
   all-purpose flour
½ teaspoon baking powder
a pinch of salt
60 g/4 tablespoons butter,
   cubed and soft
100 g/½ cup packed dark
   brown sugar
50 g/¼ cup (caster) sugar
½ teaspoon vanilla extract
1 egg
100 ml/⅓ cup milk

PECAN PIE FILLING
80 ml/⅓ cup liquid glucose
   or light corn syrup
1 tablespoon honey
1 egg, beaten
45 g/3 tablespoons butter,
   melted
½ teaspoon vanilla extract
50 g/¼ cup (caster) sugar
3 tablespoons plain/
   all-purpose flour
3 tablespoons pecans,
   plus extra to decorate
40 g/1½ oz. milk chocolate

CARAMEL BUTTERCREAM
100 g/6½ tablespoons
   butter, cubed and soft
3 tablespoons storebought
   caramel sauce
1 teaspoon vanilla extract
a pinch of salt
300 g/2¼ cups icing/
   confectioners' sugar
1 tablespoon milk

16-cm/7-in. cake pan
muffin pan lined with
   12 muffin cases

MAKES 12

PECAN PIE FILLING
Start by making the pecan pie filling.

Preheat the oven to 180°C/350°F/ Gas 4 and grease the cake pan.

Put the liquid glucose or corn syrup, honey, beaten egg, melted butter and vanilla in a mixing bowl and mix with a wooden spoon. Stir in the sugar and flour. Finely chop the pecans and chocolate and stir these into the mixture.

Pour into the cake pan and bake in the preheated oven for 45 minutes, stirring gently halfway through baking. After 45 minutes, the filling should be firm to the touch and a skewer inserted in the middle should come out clean. Let cool while you make the cupcakes.

CUPCAKE MIXTURE
Sift together the flour, baking powder and salt in a bowl.

Put the butter, sugars and vanilla in a mixing bowl and beat with an electric hand mixer until pale and fluffy. Stop occasionally to scrape down the side of the bowl with a rubber spatula. Beat in the egg.

Pour in one third of the dry ingredients and beat on low speed. Add half the milk and beat well. Repeat this process, then finish with the last third of the dry ingredients.

Divide the mixture between the muffin cases. Scoop a teaspoon of the pecan pie filling out of the cake pan and gently place on top of each cupcake. Bake in the preheated oven for about 20 minutes or until well risen and a skewer inserted in the middle comes out clean. Remove from the oven and let cool completely on a wire rack before decorating.

CARAMEL BUTTERCREAM
While the cupcakes are cooling down, make the caramel buttercream.

Put the butter, caramel sauce, vanilla and salt in a mixing bowl and beat with an electric hand mixer on medium speed until creamy.

Gradually add half the sugar, beating on low speed. Beat in the milk, then the remaining sugar and beat well.

Spread the frosting over the cold cupcakes using a spatula, or spoon the frosting into a piping bag fitted with a star nozzle/tip and pipe it on top of the cupcakes. Pour some chopped pecans into a saucer and roll the edge of each cupcake in the pecans to coat.

LOLA'S IS VERY PROUD TO SUPPORT GREAT ORMOND STREET HOSPITAL FOR CHILDREN IN LONDON. THIS CUPCAKE WAS CREATED BY FOUR-YEAR-OLD JESSICA, A FORMER PATIENT. IT HAS BEEN ONE OF OUR BEST-SELLERS AND SUPPORTED THE HOSPITAL'S 'KISS IT BETTER' CAMPAIGN.

VANILLA CHOCOLATE RAINBOW

175 g/1⅓ cups plain/
   all-purpose flour
1 teaspoon baking powder
a pinch of salt
150 g/1 stick plus
   2 tablespoons butter,
   cubed and soft
150 g/¾ cup (caster) sugar
½ vanilla pod/bean
3 eggs
150 g/1¼ cups milk
   chocolate chips

RAINBOW
BUTTERCREAM
120 g/1 stick butter, cubed
   and soft
1 teaspoon vanilla extract
500 g/3⅔ cups icing/
   confectioners' sugar
1 tablespoon milk
red, yellow and blue food
   colouring (optional)

TO DECORATE
multi-coloured candies and
   chocolate flakes (optional)
edible glitter

muffin pan lined with
   12 muffin cases or mini-
   cupcake pan lined with
   24 mini-cupcake cases

MAKES 12 REGULAR
OR 24 TINY

Preheat the oven to 180°C/350°F/Gas 4.

Sift together the flour, baking powder and salt in a bowl.

Put the butter and sugar in a mixing bowl and beat with an electric hand mixer until pale and fluffy. Stop occasionally to scrape down the side of the bowl with a rubber spatula. Using a small, sharp knife, slit the vanilla pod/bean down its length and scrape the seeds out into the mixing bowl. Add the eggs, one at a time, beating well after each addition.

Slowly add the sifted dry ingredients and chocolate chips and beat on low speed until combined.

Divide the mixture between the muffin cases. Bake in the preheated oven for 20–25 minutes for regular cupcakes, or a little less for tiny cupcakes. They should well risen and a skewer inserted in the middle should come out clean. Remove from the oven and let cool completely on a wire rack before decorating.

RAINBOW BUTTERCREAM
While the cupcakes are cooling down, make the rainbow buttercream.

Put the butter in a bowl and beat with an electric hand mixer until very soft and smooth. Stir in the vanilla. Sift the sugar into the bowl in 4 batches, beating until incorporated and the frosting is smooth. Add the milk and beat again.

If you want to make the buttercream rainbow-coloured, divide it between 3 bowls and tint each a different colour using the food colourings. Using a piping bag fitted with a star nozzle/tip spoon a portion of each colour of buttercream into the bag, layering it until you have used up all the buttercream. Slowly start to squeeze the bag onto a plate until the rainbow effect begins.

Pipe the rainbow buttercream onto the cold cupcakes. Alternatively, spread undyed buttercream onto the cold cupcakes with a spatula. Cover the cupcakes with multi-coloured candies and finish with a flaked chocolate. Either way, dust with edible glitter.

LOLA'S RAINBOW VELVET CUPCAKE WAS CREATED TO CELEBRATE THE 'RAINBOW NATION', A TERM COINED BY ARCHBISHOP DESMOND TUTU TO DESCRIBE POST-APARTHEID SOUTH AFRICA AFTER ITS FIRST FULLY DEMOCRATIC ELECTION IN 1994. THE TOPPING HIDES A TINTED CUPCAKE BASE – YOU WON'T KNOW WHAT COLOUR YOU'VE GOT UNTIL YOU TAKE THE FIRST BITE! THESE ARE A TRIBUTE TO VICTORIA AND ROMY'S ROOTS, WHICH LIE IN THE HEART OF SOUTH AFRICA.

RAINBOW VELVET

- 250 g/2 cups self-rising flour
- 1 teaspoon baking powder
- 150 g/¾ cup (caster) sugar
- 180 ml/¾ cup vegetable oil
- 2 eggs
- 1 teaspoon white wine vinegar
- ½ teaspoon vanilla extract
- 140 g/½ cup plain yogurt
- 3 tablespoons milk
- assorted food colouring
- sprinkles, to decorate

MASCARPONE FROSTING
- 80 g/5 tablespoons butter, cubed and soft
- 150 g/⅔ cup mascarpone
- 150 g/5 oz. cream cheese
- 100 g/¾ cup icing/ confectioners' sugar

muffin pan lined with 12 muffin cases

MAKES 12

Preheat the oven to 180°C/350°F/Gas 4.

Sift together the flour and baking powder in a bowl.

Put the sugar, oil, eggs, vinegar and vanilla in a mixing bowl and beat with an electric hand mixer until light.

Add the sifted dry ingredients and beat until combined. Mix the yogurt and milk together, then add to the mixing bowl. Beat until mixed and add a little more milk or yogurt if the mixture looks too dry.

Divide the batter between as many bowls as food colouring you are using. Tint each one a different colour, then divide the mixture between the muffin cases (just one colour per case).

Bake in the preheated oven for 20–25 minutes or until well risen and a skewer inserted in the middle comes out clean. Remove from the oven and let cool completely on a wire rack before decorating.

MASCARPONE FROSTING
While the cupcakes are cooling down, make the mascarpone frosting.

Put the butter, mascarpone and cream cheese in a mixing bowl and beat with an electric hand mixer. Beat in the sugar until thick and creamy.

Spread the frosting over the cold cupcakes using a spatula. Pour sprinkles into a saucer and roll the tops of the cupcakes in the sprinkles to coat.

LOLA'S BAKERY MANAGER KEITH ORIGINALLY CREATED THIS INCREDIBLE CUPCAKE FOR VICTORIA'S WEDDING DESSERT DISPLAY. IT'S A DREAMY BLEND OF MACADAMIA PRALINE ON TOP OF OUR NOW-FAMOUS SMOOTH WHITE CHOCOLATE CHEESECAKE. IT WAS SO WELL RECEIVED THAT WE THOUGHT IT ONLY FAIR TO SHARE...

MACADAMIA WHITE CHOCOLATE CHEESECAKE

BASE
100 g/3½ oz. digestive biscuits/graham crackers or shortbread cookies, crushed
1½ tablespoons butter, melted

FILLING
130 g/4½ oz. white chocolate, finely chopped
160 g/5½ oz. cream cheese
140 g/generous ½ cup mascarpone
2½ tablespoons (caster) sugar
1 teaspoon vanilla extract
2 eggs
2 tablespoons sour cream

MACADAMIA PRALINE
210 g/1⅓ cups shelled macadamia nuts
210 g/1 cup (caster) sugar
20 g/4 teaspoons butter

muffin pan lined with 12 muffin cases
baking sheet lined with non-stick parchment paper

MAKES 12

Preheat the oven to 170°C/325°F/Gas 3.

BASE
Mix the crushed digestive biscuits/graham crackers with the melted butter. Place about a teaspoon of this into each muffin case – enough to cover the base of the case. Press down slightly with the back of the spoon.

FILLING
Put the chocolate in a heatproof bowl over a pan of simmering water. Do not let the base of the bowl touch the water. Heat, stirring, until the chocolate melts. Remove from the heat and set aside.

Put the cream cheese, mascarpone, sugar and vanilla in a mixing bowl and beat with an electric hand mixer on medium speed.

Add the eggs, one at a time, and beat between each addition. Reduce the speed to low and slowly add the melted chocolate, then increase the speed to medium to finish beating. Finally, stir in the sour cream.

Transfer the mixture to a jug/pitcher and pour into the muffin cases over the bases. Bake in the preheated oven for 20–25 minutes or until set and just firm

to the touch. The cakes will rise and feel springy.

Remove from the oven and let cool for about 30 minutes in the muffin pan. They will sink slightly during this time. Carefully remove from the muffin pan and refrigerate the cupcakes for at least 3 hours or overnight before applying the praline topping.

MACADAMIA PRALINE
Preheat the oven to 170°C/325°F/Gas 3.

Put the macadamias on a baking sheet and roast in the preheated oven for 5–10 minutes.

Meanwhile, scatter the sugar evenly over the base of a heavy-based saucepan and set over medium heat. Do not stir. When it has melted and starts to turn an amber colour, remove from the heat and add the butter and roasted nuts. Pour onto the prepared, lined baking sheet.

As soon as the mixture has cooled down and set, chop it into chunks with a sharp knife.

Put a chunk of the praline on top of each chilled cupcake.

These cheesecake cupcakes will keep in the refrigerator for 3–4 days.

THE TEXTURE, FLAVOUR AND CREAMINESS OF THESE CHEESECAKES ARE TO DIE FOR. THEY ARE BASED ON ONE OF OUR FAVOURITE SOUTH AFRICAN RECIPES AND COMBINE CRUMB BASE, WHITE AND MILK CHOCOLATE CREAM CHEESE FILLING AND A BOUNTY OF BROWNIE, CHOCOLATE BUTTONS AND MELTED WHITE CHOCOLATE ON TOP. THEY LAST MUCH LONGER THAN A NORMAL CUPCAKE (IN THE FRIDGE).

CHOCOLATE CHEESECAKE

BASE
100 g/3½ oz. digestive biscuits/graham crackers or shortbread cookies, crushed
1½ tablespoons butter, melted

FILLING
130 g/4½ oz. white chocolate, finely chopped
130 g/4½ oz. milk chocolate, finely chopped
160 g/5½ oz. cream cheese
140 g/generous ½ cup mascarpone
2½ tablespoons (caster) sugar
1 teaspoon vanilla extract
2 eggs
2 tablespoons sour cream

TO DECORATE
brownies, chopped
milk chocolate buttons
white chocolate buttons
white chocolate, melted

muffin pan lined with 12 muffin cases

MAKES 12

Preheat the oven to 170°C/325°F/ Gas 3.

BASE
Mix the crushed digestive biscuits/ graham crackers with the melted butter. Place about a teaspoon of this into each muffin case – enough to cover the base of the case. Press down slightly with the back of the spoon.

FILLING
Put the white and milk chocolates together in a heatproof bowl over a pan of simmering water. Do not let the base of the bowl touch the water. Heat, stirring, until the chocolate melts. Remove from the heat and set aside.

Put the cream cheese, mascarpone, sugar and vanilla in a mixing bowl and beat with an electric hand mixer on medium speed.

Add the eggs, one at a time, and beat between each addition. Reduce the speed to low and slowly add the

melted chocolate, then increase the speed to medium to finish beating. Finally, stir in the sour cream.

Transfer the mixture to a jug/pitcher and pour into the muffin cases over the bases. Bake in the preheated oven for 20–25 minutes or until set and just firm to the touch. The cakes will rise and feel springy.

Remove from the oven and let cool for about 30 minutes in the muffin pan. They will sink slightly during this time.

Carefully remove the cupcakes from the muffin pan and refrigerate them for at least 3 hours or overnight to allow them time to set before applying the assorted toppings.

TO DECORATE
Top each chilled cupcake with chunks of chopped brownie, milk and white chocolate buttons and a drizzle of melted white chocolate.

These cheesecake cupcakes will keep in the refrigerator for 3–4 days.

LOLA'S STICKY TOFFEE CUPCAKE WAS INSPIRED BY THE CLASSIC
BRITISH DESSERT AND DEVISED TO CELEBRATE ST GEORGE'S DAY. MADE
WITH CHOPPED DATES AND TOPPED WITH A SINFULLY SWEET RUM
TOFFEE GANACHE, IT'S IDEAL WITH A SCOOP OF VANILLA ICE CREAM.

STICKY TOFFEE

180 g/1 generous cup
    chopped pitted dates
2 tablespoons golden syrup
    or light corn syrup
130 ml/½ cup boiling
    water
200 g/1⅔ cups self-rising
    flour
1 teaspoon baking powder
100 g/7 tablespoons
    butter, cubed and soft
160 g/¾ cup muscovado
    sugar
2 eggs
1 teaspoon vanilla extract
vanilla ice cream, to serve
fan wafers, to decorate

RUM TOFFEE GANACHE
200 g/1 cup (caster) sugar
50 g/3 tablespoons butter,
    cubed
150 ml/⅔ cup double/
    heavy cream
2 teaspoons dark rum
300 g/10 oz. white
    chocolate, chopped
200 g/1½ cups icing/
    confectioners' sugar

*muffin pan lined with
    12 muffin cases*

MAKES 12

Preheat the oven to 190°C/375°F/
Gas 5.
    Put the chopped dates, golden syrup
or corn syrup and boiling water in a
bowl and let soak until the water has
cooled to room temperature.
    Meanwhile, sift the flour and baking
powder together in a bowl.
    Put the butter and sugar in a mixing
bowl and beat with an electric hand
mixer until pale and fluffy. Stop
occasionally to scrape down the side
of the bowl with a rubber spatula. Add
the eggs, one at a time, beating well
after each addition. Add the vanilla.
    Break up the dates gently with
a fork. Slowly add the sifted dry
ingredients and the date mixture to
the mixing bowl and beat on low
speed until combined.
    Divide the mixture between the
muffin cases. Bake in the preheated
oven for 15–20 minutes or until well
risen and a skewer inserted in the
middle comes out clean. Remove from
the oven and let cool completely on
a wire rack before decorating.

RUM TOFFEE GANACHE
While the cupcakes are cooling down,
make the rum toffee ganache.
    Scatter the (caster) sugar evenly over
the base of a heavy-based saucepan
and set over medium heat. Do not stir.
When it has melted and starts to turn
an amber colour, remove from the heat
and add the butter. Add 3 tablespoons
of the cream and the rum and whisk
thoroughly with a balloon whisk until
well mixed. Let cool to room temperature.
    Put the remaining cream in a
saucepan over medium heat and heat
until just starting to bubble around the
edges. Remove from the heat and stir
in the chocolate. Stir until the chocolate
has melted and you have a glossy
ganache. Let cool to room temperature.
    When both the rum sauce and white
chocolate ganache have cooled, mix
them together, then add the icing/
confectioners' sugar. Mix until smooth.
Refrigerate for 10 minutes.
    Spread the ganache over the cold
cupcakes using a spatula. Top with a
spoonful of vanilla ice cream and finish
with a fan wafer. Serve immediately.

WHETHER YOU CALL THEM TOFFEE OR CANDY APPLES (OR 'POMMES D'AMOUR' IN FRANCE!), THEY MAKE GREAT CUPCAKES AND THEY'RE ONE OF OUR FAVOURITE TREATS. SPREAD THE FROSTING IN A DOME SHAPE TO RESEMBLE AN APPLE, AND FINISH WITH POPSICLE STICKS!

TOFFEE APPLE

200 g/1½ cups plain/
    all-purpose flour
½ teaspoon baking powder
a pinch of salt
130 g/1 stick plus
    2 teaspoons butter,
    cubed and soft
130 g/⅔ cup light
    muscovado sugar
2 eggs
85 g/6 tablespoons
    storebought toffee fudge
    /butterscotch caramel
    sauce
2 peeled and grated
    Bramley or Granny Smith
    apples, plus extra slices
    to decorate
about 1 tablespoon milk

TOFFEE BUTTERCREAM
75 g/5 tablespoons butter,
    cubed and soft
500 g/3⅔ cups icing/
    confectioners' sugar
1 teaspoon vanilla extract
3 tablespoons storebought
    toffee fudge/butterscotch
    caramel sauce, plus extra
    to drizzle

*muffin pan lined with
    12 muffin cases
lollipop/popsicle sticks,
    to decorate (optional)*

MAKES 12

Preheat the oven to 190°C/375°F/
Gas 5.

Sift together the flour, baking
powder and salt in a bowl.

Put the butter and sugar in a mixing
bowl and beat with an electric hand
mixer until pale and fluffy. Stop
occasionally to scrape down the side
of the bowl with a rubber spatula. Add
the eggs, one at a time, beating well
after each addition. Add the toffee
fudge/butterscotch caramel sauce.

Slowly add the sifted dry ingredients
and grated apple and beat on low
speed until combined. If the mixture
seems too thick, add a little milk.

Divide the mixture between the
muffin cases. Bake in the preheated
oven for 20–25 minutes or until well
risen and a skewer inserted in the
middle comes out clean. Remove from
the oven and let cool completely on
a wire rack before decorating.

TOFFEE BUTTERCREAM
While the cupcakes are cooling down,
make the toffee buttercream.

Put the butter in a bowl and beat
with an electric hand mixer until very
soft and smooth. Add one third of the
sugar, beat, then add the vanilla. Beat
in another third of the sugar, then the
toffee fudge/butterscotch caramel
sauce. Finally, beat in the remaining
sugar. Add about 1 or 2 tablespoons
of water if the mixture seems too stiff.

Spread the frosting over the cold
cupcakes using a spatula, making it
into a neat dome shape. Top with a thin
apple wedge, drizzle with more toffee
fudge/butterscotch caramel sauce and
stick a couple of lollipop/popsicle sticks
(if using) in the cupcake to resemble
toffee apples.

LOLA'S SALTED CARAMEL CUPCAKE IS OUR TAKE ON A TRADITIONAL FRENCH TREAT. FOR THIS SALTY-SWEET CREATION, WE HAVE SPECIALLY CHOSEN FLEUR DE SEL, WHICH IS HAND-HARVESTED SEA SALT COLLECTED ALONG THE COAST OF BRITTANY IN FRANCE.

SALTED CARAMEL

250 g/2 cups plain/
   all-purpose flour
1 teaspoon baking powder
¼ teaspoon salt
125 g/1 stick butter, cubed
   and soft
185 g/1 scant cup packed
   light brown sugar
1 teaspoon vanilla extract
2 eggs
150 ml/⅔ cup buttermilk
12 salted caramel chocolates
fleur de sel, to sprinkle

SALTED CARAMEL
FILLING
180 g/1 scant cup (caster)
   sugar
90 g/6 tablespoons butter
120 ml/½ cup double/
   heavy cream

SALTED CARAMEL
FROSTING
250 g/2 sticks butter,
   cubed and soft
3 tablespoons storebought
   toffee fudge/butterscotch
   caramel sauce
750 g/5½ cups icing/
   confectioners' sugar
75 ml/⅓ cup milk
a pinch of salt

*muffin pan lined with
   12 muffin cases*

MAKES 12

Preheat the oven to 180°C/350°F/Gas 4.

Sift together the flour, baking powder and salt in a bowl.

Put the butter, sugar and vanilla in a mixing bowl and beat with an electric hand mixer until pale and fluffy. Stop occasionally to scrape down the side of the bowl with a rubber spatula.

Add the eggs, one at a time, beating well after each addition. Add the sifted dry ingredients and buttermilk in alternate batches and beat on low speed until combined.

Divide the mixture between the muffin cases. Bake in the preheated oven for about 25 minutes or until well risen and a skewer inserted in the middle comes out clean. Remove from the oven and let cool completely on a wire rack before decorating.

SALTED CARAMEL FILLING
Scatter the sugar evenly over the base of a heavy-based saucepan and set over medium heat. Do not stir. When it has melted and starts to turn an amber colour, remove from the heat and add the butter. Add the cream and whisk thoroughly with a balloon whisk until well mixed. Let cool.

SALTED CARAMEL FROSTING
While the cupcakes are cooling down, make the salted caramel frosting.

Put the butter in a bowl and beat with an electric hand mixer until very soft and smooth. Add the toffee fudge/butterscotch caramel sauce, followed by the sugar. Beat on low speed, then gradually add the milk until well combined. Turn the speed up to high, add the salt and beat for 1 minute.

When the cupcakes are completely cold, make a hole in the middle by scooping out a neat portion of the cake with a teaspoon. Fill the hole with a dollop of the salted caramel filling. Put the portion of cake back on top of the filling.

Spread the frosting over the cupcakes using a spatula, or spoon the frosting into a piping bag fitted with a star nozzle/tip and pipe it on top of the cupcakes. Top with a salted caramel chocolate and sprinkle a little fleur de sel over it.

NOTE
You can find fleur de sel at well-stocked supermarkets and gourmet stores.

OUR INSPIRATION FOR LOLA'S CINNAMON TWIST CAME FROM THE FAMOUS SNICKERDOODLE, A COOKIE ROLLED IN CINNAMON SUGAR. JUST LIKE THE COOKIE, OUR MELT-IN-YOUR-MOUTH CUPCAKE GIVES WAY TO A SOFT, SUBTLY SWEET, AND POSITIVELY SCRUMPTIOUS CINNAMON CAKE CENTRE. THE CINNAMON BUTTERCREAM IS UTTERLY DREAMY.

CINNAMON TWIST

175 g/1⅓ cups plain/
   all-purpose flour
1 teaspoon baking powder
2 teaspoons ground
   cinnamon
a pinch of salt
150 g/1 stick plus
   2 tablespoons butter,
   cubed and soft
150 g/¾ cup (caster) sugar
½ vanilla pod/bean
3 eggs
65 g/½ cup raisins
65 g/½ cup chopped
   pecans
cinnamon sticks, to top
chopped snickerdoodles,
   to top

CINNAMON
BUTTERCREAM
120 g/1 stick butter, cubed
   and soft
500 g/3⅔ cups icing/
   confectioners' sugar
1 teaspoon vanilla extract
1 teaspoon ground
   cinnamon
1 tablespoon milk

*muffin pan lined with
   12 muffin cases*

MAKES 12

Preheat the oven to 180°C/350°F/ Gas 4.
   Sift together the flour, baking powder, ground cinnamon and salt in a bowl.
   Put the butter and sugar in a mixing bowl and beat with an electric hand mixer until pale and fluffy. Stop occasionally to scrape down the side of the bowl with a rubber spatula. Using a small, sharp knife, slit the vanilla pod/bean down its length and scrape the seeds out into the mixing bowl. Add the eggs, one at a time, beating well after each addition.
   Slowly add the sifted dry ingredients, raisins and pecans and beat on low speed until combined.
   Divide the mixture between the muffin cases. Bake in the preheated oven for 20–25 minutes or until well risen and a skewer inserted in the

middle comes out clean. Remove from the oven and let cool completely on a wire rack before decorating.

CINNAMON BUTTERCREAM
While the cupcakes are cooling down, make the cinnamon buttercream.
   Put the butter in a bowl and beat with an electric hand mixer until very soft and smooth. Sift half the sugar into the bowl, beating until incorporated. Add the second half of the sugar and beat on low speed. Add the vanilla and cinnamon. Slowly pour in the milk and when it is mixed in, beat for 3–5 minutes on a higher speed.
   Spread the frosting over the cold cupcakes using a spatula, or spoon the frosting into a piping bag fitted with a star nozzle/tip and pipe it on top of the cupcakes. Top with cinnamon sticks and chunks of snickerdoodle.

LET'S HAVE A CUPPA

AS BREAKFAST OPTIONS GO, LOLA'S MASALA CHAI TEA CUPCAKE IS TOP OF OUR LIST, AND YOU GET A WHOLE HOST OF HEALTH BENEFITS, TOO! CHAI TEA CONTAINS, AMONG OTHERS, GINGER, WHICH HAS ANTI-INFLAMMATORY PROPERTIES, CINNAMON, WHICH HELPS REGULATE BLOOD SUGARS, AND NUTMEG, WHICH PROMOTES BETTER DIGESTION.

MASALA CHAI TEA

175 ml/¾ cup milk
2 bags of chai tea
250 g/2 cups plain/
   all-purpose flour
½ teaspoon baking powder
¼ teaspoon bicarbonate
   of/baking soda
¼ teaspoon salt
1 teaspoon ground
   cinnamon
½ teaspoon ground
   cardamom
¼ teaspoon ground ginger
a pinch of ground cloves
110 g/7½ tablespoons
   butter, cubed and soft
200 g/1 cup (caster) sugar
1 teaspoon vanilla extract
2 eggs
hot chocolate powder,
   to dust

CHAI BUTTERCREAM
110 g/7½ tablespoons
   butter, cubed and soft
260 g/2 cups icing/
   confectioners' sugar
1 teaspoon vanilla extract
1 teaspoon ground
   cinnamon
1 teaspoon ground ginger
about 1 teaspoon milk

*muffin pan lined with
   12 muffin cases*

MAKES 12

Preheat the oven to 180°C/350°F/Gas 4.

To make chai tea, put the milk in a small saucepan and heat gently. Drop in the teabags and let infuse while you start making the cupcake mixture.

Sift together the flour, baking powder, bicarbonate of/baking soda, salt, ground cinnamon, cardamom, ginger and cloves in a bowl.

Put the butter, sugar and vanilla in a mixing bowl and beat with an electric hand mixer until pale and fluffy. Stop occasionally to scrape down the side of the bowl with a rubber spatula. Add the eggs, one at a time, beating well after each addition.

Discard the teabags from the chai-infused milk. Pour one third of the sifted dry ingredients into the mixture and beat on low speed. Add half the chai-infused milk and beat well. Repeat this process, then finish with the last third of the dry ingredients.

Divide the mixture between the muffin cases. Bake in the preheated oven for 23–25 minutes or until well risen and a skewer inserted in the middle comes out clean. Remove from the oven and let cool completely on a wire rack before decorating.

CHAI BUTTERCREAM
While the cupcakes are cooling down, make the chai buttercream.

Put the butter in a bowl and beat with an electric hand mixer until very soft and smooth. Sift half the sugar into the bowl, beating until incorporated. Add the second half of the sugar and beat on low speed. Add the vanilla, ground cinnamon and ginger. Beat for 3–5 minutes on a higher speed. Add a little milk, if necessary, to loosen.

Spread the frosting over the cold cupcakes using a spatula. Dust the tops with hot chocolate powder, using a heart-shape stencil if you have one.

NOTE
Chai tea bags are available through the Tazo and Dragonfly brands, among others. If you cannot find these, then substitute 4 teaspoons powdered instant chai latte, which is widely available, and whisk it directly into the warm milk.

IN ITALY AND THROUGHOUT CONTINENTAL EUROPE, CAPPUCCINO IS TRADITIONALLY CONSUMED WITH SOME KIND OF SWEET PASTRY. WE CREATED LOLA'S CAPPUCCINO WAFER CUPCAKE TO GIVE YOU THE BEST OF BOTH WORLDS! THE CAKE IS INFUSED WITH THE RICH AROMA OF ESPRESSO AND TOPPED WITH A MILKY COFFEE FROSTING. IT IS FINISHED WITH A DELICIOUSLY CRISP WAFER.

CAPPUCCINO WAFER

130 g/1 cup self-rising flour
1 teaspoon baking powder
100 g/⅔ cup ground almonds
130 g/1 stick plus 2 teaspoons butter
180 g/1 cup plus 2 tablespoons (caster) sugar
1 teaspoon vanilla extract
2 eggs
70 g/5 tablespoons crème fraîche
1 teaspoon ground espresso
¾ teaspoon Amaretto
fan wafers, to decorate
grated chocolate, to top

COFFEE MASCARPONE FROSTING
375 g/1 cup plus 5 tablespoons mascarpone
2 teaspoons ground espresso mixed with 3½ tablespoons boiling water, or 2 double shots of espresso
200 g/1½ cups icing/ confectioners' sugar
2 teaspoons vanilla extract

muffin pan lined with 12 muffin cases

MAKES 12

Preheat the oven to 180°C/350°F/ Gas 4.

Sift together the flour and baking powder in a bowl. Stir in the almonds.

Put the butter, sugar and vanilla in a mixing bowl and beat with an electric hand mixer until pale and fluffy. Stop occasionally to scrape down the side of the bowl with a rubber spatula. Add the eggs, one at a time, beating well after each addition.

Slowly add the dry ingredients, then the crème fraîche, ground espresso and Amaretto and beat on low speed until combined.

Divide the mixture between the muffin cases. Bake in the preheated oven for 20–25 minutes or until well risen and a skewer inserted in the middle comes out clean. Remove from the oven and let cool completely on a wire rack before decorating.

COFFEE MASCARPONE FROSTING

While the cupcakes are cooling down, make the coffee mascarpone frosting.

Put all the ingredients in a mixing bowl and beat with an electric hand mixer until stiff peaks form. Do not overbeat. Refrigerate for 2–3 hours, or until firm enough to pipe.

Spread the frosting over the cold cupcakes using a spatula, or spoon the frosting into a piping bag fitted with a large, plain nozzle/tip and pipe it on top of the cupcakes. Scatter grated chocolate over the top and finish with a piece of fan wafer.

NOTHING TASTES MORE LIKE CHRISTMAS THAN LOLA'S DELICIOUS
GINGERBREAD LATTE CUPCAKE – NOT TOO LIGHT, NOT TOO DENSE –
AND COMPLEMENTED WITH A COFFEE CINNAMON TOPPING.

GINGERBREAD LATTE

120 g/½ cup golden syrup
  or light corn syrup
120 g/½ cup black
  treacle/dark molasses
200 ml/¾ cup double/
  heavy cream
250 g/2 cups plain/
  all-purpose flour
2 teaspoons baking powder
1½ tablespoons cocoa
  powder
1 teaspoon ground espresso
2 teaspoons ground ginger
½ teaspoon ground allspice
½ teaspoon ground nutmeg
¼ teaspoon salt
135 g/1 stick butter, cubed
  and soft
125 g/⅔ cup packed dark
  brown sugar
2 eggs
gingerbread-men sugar
  sprinkles, to decorate

COFFEE CINNAMON
BUTTERCREAM

120 g/1 stick butter, cubed
  and soft
1 teaspoon vanilla extract
500 g/3⅔ cups icing/
  confectioners' sugar
3 tablespoons milk
2 teaspoons ground espresso
  and 1 teaspoon ground
  cinnamon mixed with
  ½ teaspoon hot water

*muffin pan lined with
  12 muffin cases*

MAKES 12

Preheat the oven to 180°C/350°F/
Gas 4.

Put the golden syrup or corn syrup,
treacle/molasses and cream in a
saucepan and heat gently until just
melted and well mixed. Do not allow
to come to a boil.

Sift together the flour, baking
powder, cocoa powder, ground
espresso, ginger, allspice, nutmeg
and salt in a bowl.

Put the butter and sugar in a mixing
bowl and beat with an electric hand
mixer until pale and fluffy. Stop
occasionally to scrape down the side
of the bowl with a rubber spatula. Add
the eggs, one at a time, beating well
after each addition.

Beat in one third of the melted syrup
mixture and one third of the sifted dry
ingredients. (This will prevent the mixture
from curdling.) Now add the remaining
syrup mixture and dry ingredients and
beat until well mixed.

Divide the mixture between the
muffin cases. Bake in the preheated
oven for 25–30 minutes or until well
risen and a skewer inserted in the
middle comes out clean. Remove from
the oven and let cool completely on
a wire rack before decorating.

COFFEE CINNAMON
BUTTERCREAM

While the cupcakes are cooling down,
make the coffee cinnamon buttercream.

Put the butter in a bowl and beat
with an electric hand mixer until very
soft and smooth. Stir in the vanilla. Sift
half the icing/confectioners' sugar into
the bowl, beating until incorporated.
Add the second half of the sugar and
beat on low speed. Slowly pour in the
milk and when it is mixed in, beat for
3–5 minutes on a higher speed. Add the
espresso-cinnamon paste and beat in.

Spread the frosting over the cold
cupcakes using a spatula, or spoon the
frosting into a piping bag fitted with
a star nozzle/tip and pipe it on top of
the cupcakes. Top with gingerbread-men
sugar sprinkles.

NOTE
Gingerbread-men sugar sprinkles can
be bought from these and other online
cake-decorating suppliers:
www.sugarcraft.com
www.cakescookiesandcraftsshop.co.uk

AT LOLA'S, WE LOVE BAKING WITH MATCHA – A FINELY GROUND, HIGH-QUALITY JAPANESE GREEN TEA. IT HAS TO BE THE REAL THING AND SHOULDN'T BE CONFUSED WITH REGULAR GREEN TEA POWDER. POUND FOR POUND, MATCHA CONTAINS HIGHER LEVELS OF ANTIOXIDANTS THAN BLUEBERRIES, GOJIBERRIES AND POMEGRANATES, IT BOOSTS THE METABOLISM AND REDUCES CHOLESTEROL, SO WHAT'S NOT TO LOVE?

CHOCOLATE MATCHA

150 g/1 cup plus 3 tablespoons self-rising flour
2½ tablespoons cocoa powder, plus extra to dust
¼ teaspoon matcha powder
1 teaspoon baking powder
a pinch of salt
150 g/1 stick plus 2 tablespoons butter
265 g/1⅓ cups (caster) sugar
120 g/4 oz. dark/bittersweet chocolate (70% cocoa), chopped
1 egg

MATCHA BUTTERCREAM
1 tablespoon single/light cream
½ teaspoon matcha powder
125 g/1 stick butter, cubed and soft
500 g/3⅔ cups icing/confectioners' sugar

muffin pan lined with 12 muffin cases

MAKES 12

Preheat the oven to 180°C/350°F/Gas 4.

Sift together the flour, cocoa powder, matcha powder, baking powder and salt in a bowl.

Put the butter, sugar and chocolate in a medium saucepan over low heat and heat until melted and smooth. Add 150 ml/⅔ cup water and whisk with a balloon whisk until combined. Let cool for a few minutes.

Add the egg to the saucepan and whisk in. Finally, whisk in the sifted dry ingredients and mix well.

Divide the mixture between the muffin cases. Bake in the preheated oven for 25–30 minutes or until well risen and a skewer inserted in the middle comes out clean. Remove from the oven and let cool completely on a wire rack before decorating.

MATCHA BUTTERCREAM
While the cupcakes are cooling down, make the matcha buttercream.

Mix the cream and matcha powder to make a paste.

Put the butter in a bowl and beat with an electric hand mixer until very soft and smooth. Sift half the sugar into the bowl, beating until incorporated. Add the second half of the sugar and beat on low speed. Add the cream-matcha paste and mix well.

Spread the frosting over the cold cupcakes using a spatula, or spoon the frosting into a piping bag fitted with a large, plain nozzle/tip and pipe it on top of the cupcakes. Dust lightly with cocoa powder.

NOTE
Matcha powder is not easily available but Japanese grocers and specialty tea shops will stock it.

HOT CHOCOLATE BECAME POPULAR IN EUROPE AFTER BEING INTRODUCED FROM MEXICO, WHERE IT IS SERVED ALONGSIDE A VARIETY OF MEXICAN PASTRIES SUCH AS *PAN DULCE* AND *CHURROS*. WHEN YOU BITE INTO THIS DARK CHOCOLATE CAKE, THE PEPPERMINT FILLING MELTS ON YOUR TONGUE, CREATING A DELICIOUSLY SMOOTH MINT HOT CHOCOLATE SENSATION! GO ON, INDULGE YOURSELF.

MINT HOT CHOCOLATE

100 g/3½ oz. dark/
  bittersweet chocolate
  (70% cocoa), chopped
175 g/1 stick plus
  5 tablespoons butter,
  cubed and soft
225 g/1 cup plus 2
  tablespoons (caster) sugar
4 eggs
100 g/¾ cup self-rising
  flour
3 tablespoons cocoa powder
a pinch of salt
12 small after-dinner mints

MINT FILLING
250 g/1¾ cups icing/
  confectioners' sugar
2 teaspoons peppermint
  extract

MINT BUTTERCREAM
120 g/1 stick butter, cubed
  and soft
500 g/3⅔ cups icing/
  confectioners' sugar
1 teaspoon mint extract
1 teaspoon vanilla extract
1 tablespoon milk
green food colouring

*muffin pan lined with
  12 muffin cases*

MAKES 12

Preheat the oven to 180°C/350°F/
Gas 4.

Put the chocolate and butter in a heatproof bowl over a pan of simmering water. Do not let the base of the bowl touch the water. Heat, stirring, until the chocolate melts and you have a smooth, glossy mixture. Remove from the heat and stir in the sugar. Let cool for about 10 minutes.

Now beat with an electric hand mixer for 3 minutes. Add the eggs, one at a time, beating for 10 seconds between each addition. Sift the flour, cocoa and salt into the bowl and beat until blended.

Divide the mixture between the muffin cases. Bake in the preheated oven for about 25 minutes or until well risen and a skewer inserted in the middle comes out clean. Remove from the oven and let cool completely on a wire rack before decorating.

MINT FILLING

Sift the sugar into a small bowl. Add the peppermint extract and 1 tablespoon water and mix with a balloon whisk. Add another tablespoon of water and mix again. All the sugar should now be incorporated, but add a drop more water if it needs it.

MINT BUTTERCREAM

While the cupcakes are cooling down, make the mint buttercream.

Put the butter in a bowl and beat with an electric hand mixer until very soft and smooth. Sift half the sugar into the bowl, beating until incorporated. Add the second half of the sugar and beat on low speed. Add the mint and vanilla extracts. Slowly pour in the milk and, when it is mixed in, beat for 3–5 minutes on a higher speed.

Add a couple of drops of food colouring and beat until incorporated. Add more colouring if you want a richer shade of green!

When the cupcakes are completely cold, make a hole in the middle by scooping out a neat portion of the cake with a teaspoon. Fill the hole with a dollop of the mint filling. Put the portion of cake back on top of the filling.

Spread the frosting over the cupcakes using a spatula, or spoon the frosting into a piping bag fitted with a star nozzle/tip and pipe it on top of the cupcakes. Top with an after-dinner mint.

OUR ESPRESSO CUPCAKE IS STUDDED WITH DARK CHOCOLATE CHIPS, FLAVOURED WITH A HINT OF BRANDY AND TOPPED WITH AN INCREDIBLE MASCARPONE FROSTING. TIRAMISU LITERALLY MEANS 'PICK ME UP', WHICH COULDN'T DESCRIBE THE EFFECTS OF THIS CUPCAKE BETTER!

ESPRESSO TIRAMISU

400 g/3⅓ cups plain/
  all-purpose flour
4 teaspoons baking powder
1 teaspoon bicarbonate of/
  baking soda
½ teaspoon salt
2 teaspoons ground
  cinnamon
1 tablespoon ground
  espresso
275 g/1¼ cups (caster)
  sugar
120 ml/½ cup sunflower oil
150 ml/⅔ cup plain yogurt
150 ml/⅔ cup milk
2 eggs, beaten
1 tablespoon brandy
200 g/2 cups dark/
  semisweet chocolate chips
24 or 48 chocolate-coated
  coffee beans

ESPRESSO WHIP
600 ml/2½ cups double/
  heavy cream
50 g/⅓ cup icing/
  confectioners' sugar
2 teaspoons ground espresso
250 g/1 cup mascarpone

*muffin pan lined with
  12 muffin cases or mini-
  cupcake pan lined with
  24 mini cupcake cases*

MAKES 12 REGULAR
OR 24 TINY

Preheat the oven to 180°C/350°F/ Gas 4.

Sift together the flour, baking powder, bicarbonate of/baking soda, salt, ground cinnamon and ground espresso in a mixing bowl.

Put the sugar, oil, yogurt, milk, eggs, brandy and chocolate chips in another bowl and whisk well with a balloon whisk. Add this wet mixture to the sifted dry ingredients and fold in gently using a large metal spoon. Do not overmix.

Divide the mixture between the muffin cases. Smooth the tops with a spatula. Bake in the preheated oven for about 25 minutes, or a little less for tiny cupcakes. They should be well risen and a skewer inserted in the middle should come out clean. Remove from the oven and let cool completely on a wire rack before decorating.

ESPRESSO WHIP
While the cupcakes are cooling down, make the espresso whip.

Put the cream, sugar and half the ground espresso in a bowl and whisk with an electric hand mixer on medium speed until soft peaks form – don't overwhisk otherwise the cream will split or become grainy.

In a separate bowl, put the mascarpone and remaining ground espresso and whisk with the electric hand mixer until smooth. Add more coffee to taste, if you like.

Transfer a little of the whipped cream into the mascarpone mixture and fold in to loosen. Now add all the mascarpone mixture to the whipped cream and fold in gently until well mixed. Refrigerate for 1–2 hours, or until firm enough to pipe.

Spread the frosting over the cupcakes using a spatula, or spoon the frosting into a piping bag fitted with a star nozzle/tip and pipe it on top of the cupcakes. Top with 2 chocolate-covered coffee beans.

ORIGINALLY CREATED TO CELEBRATE LOLA'S FIRST CHRISTMAS IN SELFRIDGES, THIS WAS PERFECTLY NAMED BY DEON, SELFRIDGES' BAKERY BUYER AT THE TIME, THE MOMENT HE TASTED IT! IT IS A MOIST CUPCAKE INFUSED WITH DARK RUM AND STUDDED WITH DRIED FRUIT. YOU WILL NEED TO SOAK THE DRIED FRUIT THE DAY BEFORE BAKING.

BOOZY FUN

65 g/½ cup (Zante) currants
65 g/½ cup sultanas/
  golden raisins
65 g/½ cup dried
  cranberries, plus extra
225 g/1¾ cups plain/
  all-powder flour
1 teaspoon baking powder
2 teaspoons ground
  cinnamon
125 g/1 stick butter, cubed
  and soft
130 g/⅔ cup dark brown
  sugar
50 g/¼ cup (caster) sugar
2 tablespoons dark rum
2 teaspoons vanilla extract
2 eggs
2 tablespoons milk
chocolate-coated raisins,
  to decorate

CHOCOLATE BRANDY BUTTERCREAM
70 g/5 tablespoons butter,
  cubed and soft
200 g/1½ cups icing/
  confectioners' sugar
3 tablespoons cocoa powder
1 tablespoon brandy
3 tablespoons milk

*muffin pan lined with
  12 muffin cases*

MAKES 12

Put the currants, sultanas/golden raisins and dried cranberries in a bowl with 4 tablespoons boiling water and let soak overnight until plump and juicy.

The next day, preheat the oven to 180°C/350°F/Gas 4.

Sift together the flour, baking powder and cinnamon in a bowl.

Put the butter, sugars, rum and vanilla in a mixing bowl and beat with an electric hand mixer until pale and fluffy. Stop occasionally to scrape down the side of the bowl with a rubber spatula. Add the eggs, one at a time, beating well after each addition.

Gently fold in the sifted dry ingredients, then the soaked dried fruit and the milk.

Divide the mixture between the muffin cases. Bake in the preheated oven for 20–25 minutes or until well risen and a skewer inserted in the middle comes out clean. Remove from the oven and let cool completely on a wire rack before decorating.

CHOCOLATE BRANDY BUTTERCREAM
While the cupcakes are cooling down, make the chocolate brandy buttercream.

Put the butter in a bowl and beat with an electric hand mixer until very soft and smooth. Sift half the sugar and half the cocoa powder into the bowl, beating until incorporated. Add the second half of the sugar and cocoa and beat on low speed.

Add the brandy. Slowly pour in the milk and when it is mixed in, beat for 3–5 minutes on a higher speed.

Spread the frosting over the cold cupcakes using a spatula. Decorate with a cluster of dried cranberries and chocolate-coated raisins.

THE COSMOPOLITAN COCKTAIL GAINED POPULARITY IN THE 1990S, WHEN IT WAS FREQUENTLY ORDERED BY CARRIE BRADSHAW ON THE POPULAR TELEVISION SHOW, *SEX AND THE CITY*. WHEN THE *SEX AND THE CITY* MOVIE WAS RELEASED IN 2009, WE CREATED THE LOLA'S COSMO CUPCAKE TO CELEBRATE! THIS CUPCAKE IS MADE WITH LIME JUICE AND BRUSHED WITH A GRAND MARNIER GLAZE. TOPPED WITH A FLOURISH OF VODKA AND POMEGRANATE BUTTERCREAM AND A WEDGE OF LIME, THIS IS A TRULY GLAMOROUS CUPCAKE – PERFECT FOR A NIGHT IN WITH THE LADIES!

COSMO

180 g/¾ cup plus 2
   tablespoons (caster) sugar
1½ tablespoons orange
   juice
1½ tablespoons Grand
   Marnier
150 g/1 cup plus
   3 tablespoons plain/
   all-purpose flour
½ teaspoon baking powder
a pinch of salt
65 g/4½ tablespoons
   butter, cubed and soft
2 eggs
75 ml/⅓ cup milk
2 tablespoons lime juice

COSMO BUTTERCREAM
125 g/1 stick butter, cubed
   and soft
500 g/3⅔ cups icing/
   confectioners' sugar
1 teaspoon vanilla extract
1 tablespoon vodka
3 tablespoons pomegranate
   molasses
lime wedges, to decorate

*muffin pan lined with
   12 muffin cases*

MAKES 12

Preheat the oven to 180°C/350°F/
Gas 4.

To make the Grand Marnier glaze,
put 50 g/¼ cup of the sugar and the
orange juice in a small saucepan over
medium heat. Heat until the sugar has
dissolved. Add the Grand Marnier,
remove from the heat and set aside.

Sift together the flour, baking
powder and salt in a bowl.

Put the butter and the remaining
sugar in a mixing bowl and beat with
an electric hand mixer until pale and
fluffy. Stop occasionally to scrape down
the side of the bowl with a rubber
spatula. Add the eggs, one at a time,
beating well after each addition.

Mix the milk and lime juice together.
Slowly add the sifted dry ingredients,
in alternate batches with the milk
mixture, to the mixing bowl and beat
on low speed until combined.

Divide the mixture between the
muffin cases. Bake in the preheated

oven for 20–25 minutes or until well
risen and a skewer inserted in the
middle comes out clean. Remove from
the oven and let cool for 15 minutes.
Brush some of the Grand Marnier glaze
over each cupcake.

COSMO BUTTERCREAM
While the cupcakes are cooling down,
make the cosmo buttercream.

Put the butter in a bowl and beat
with an electric hand mixer until very
soft and smooth. Sift half the sugar into
the bowl, beating until incorporated.
Add the second half of the sugar and
beat on low speed. Add the vanilla,
vodka and pomegranate molasses
and beat until smooth.

Spread the frosting over the
cupcakes using a spatula, or spoon
the frosting into a piping bag fitted with
a star nozzle/tip and pipe it on top of
the cupcakes. Top with a lime wedge.

THE ONLY WAY TO FIND GOLD AT THE END OF YOUR RAINBOW ON ST PATRICK'S DAY IS WITH LOLA'S DELICIOUS CHOCOLATE CUPCAKE INFUSED WITH BAILEYS IRISH CREAM! BAILEYS IS A LIQUEUR THAT COMBINES CREAM, HONEY, COFFEE AND COCOA. IT IS ONE OF OUR FAVOURITE DRINKS AND CREATES A TRULY DECADENT DESSERT.

CHOCOLATE BAILEYS

100 g/3½ oz. milk
  chocolate, chopped
125 g/1 stick butter, cubed
220 g/1 cup plus 1
  tablespoon (caster) sugar
120 ml/½ cup Baileys
2 tablespoons whisky
1 egg
a pinch of salt
150 g/1 cup plus
  3 tablespoons plain/
  all-purpose flour
3 tablespoons cocoa
  powder
½ teaspoon baking powder
12 or 24 sugar shamrocks
edible glitter, to dust

BAILEYS BUTTERCREAM
125 g/1 stick butter, cubed
  and soft
500 g/3⅔ cups icing/
  confectioners' sugar
3 tablespoons Baileys
1 tablespoon milk

muffin pan lined with
  12 muffin cases or mini-
  cupcake pan lined with
  24 mini cupcake cases

MAKES 12 REGULAR
OR 24 TINY

Preheat the oven to 180°C/350°F/Gas 4.

Put the chocolate, butter, sugar, Baileys and whisky in a heatproof bowl over a pan of simmering water. Do not let the base of the bowl touch the water. Heat, stirring, until the chocolate melts and you have a smooth, glossy mixture. Remove from the heat and let cool for 10 minutes.

Now add the egg and salt and beat with an electric hand mixer. Sift the flour, cocoa and baking powder into the bowl and beat until blended.

Divide the mixture between the muffin cases. Bake in the preheated oven for 20–25 minutes, or a little less for tiny cupcakes. They should be well risen and a skewer inserted in the middle should come out clean. Remove from the oven and let cool completely on a wire rack before decorating.

BAILEYS BUTTERCREAM
While the cupcakes are cooling down, make the Baileys buttercream.

Put the butter in a bowl and beat with an electric hand mixer until very soft and smooth. Sift half the sugar into the bowl, beating until incorporated. Add the second half of the sugar and beat on low speed. Slowly pour in the Baileys and milk and when they are all mixed in, beat for 3–5 minutes on a higher speed.

Spread the frosting over the cold cupcakes using a spatula, or spoon the frosting into a piping bag fitted with a star nozzle/tip and pipe it on top of the cupcakes. Top with a sugar shamrock and dust with edible glitter.

NOTE
Shamrock sugar sprinkles can be bought from these and other online cake-decorating suppliers:
www.sugarcraft.com
www.cakescookiesandcraftsshop.co.uk

LOLA'S CARROT CUPCAKE EARNS A TROPICAL LABEL WITH THE ADDITION OF CRUSHED PINEAPPLE AND PECAN PIECES. THIS ENSURES THE CAKE IS UNBELIEVABLY MOIST, WITH A DELICIOUS NUTTY CRUNCH. IT IS FINISHED WITH OUR DIVINE CREAM CHEESE FROSTING, MAKING THIS LESS SWEET THAN OTHER CUPCAKES AND PERFECT ANY TIME OF THE DAY. WE THINK IT'S THE BEST CARROT CAKE YOU'LL EVER TRY.

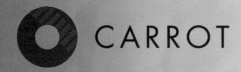 # CARROT

175 g/1⅓ cups plain/
   all-purpose flour
1 teaspoon baking powder
½ teaspoon bicarbonate
   of/baking soda
1 teaspoon ground
   cinnamon
a pinch of salt
2 eggs
200 g/1 cup (caster) sugar
100 ml/⅓ cup vegetable oil
½ teaspoon vanilla extract
2 large carrots, peeled and
   finely grated
40 g/¼ cup canned crushed
   pineapple, drained
3 tablespoons chopped
   pecans or walnuts, plus
   extra to decorate

CREAM CHEESE
FROSTING
65 g/½ stick butter, cubed
   and soft
250 g/8 oz. cream cheese
185 g/1¼ cups icing/
   confectioners' sugar

*muffin pan lined with
   12 muffin cases*

MAKES 12

Preheat the oven to 180°C/350°F/ Gas 4.

Sift together the flour, baking powder, bicarbonate of/baking soda, ground cinnamon and salt in a bowl.

Put the eggs and sugar in a mixing bowl and beat with an electric hand mixer for 5–8 minutes or until thick and pale.

Add the oil and vanilla and beat until smooth.

Add the sifted dry ingredients and beat on low speed until combined.

Stir in the carrots, pineapple and pecans and mix well.

Divide the mixture between the muffin cases. Bake in the preheated oven for 22–25 minutes or until well risen and a skewer inserted in the middle comes out clean. Remove from the oven and let cool completely on a wire rack before decorating.

CREAM CHEESE FROSTING
While the cupcakes are cooling down, make the cream cheese frosting.

Put the butter in a bowl and beat with an electric hand mixer until very soft and smooth. Add the cream cheese and beat on low speed for 2 minutes. Gradually sift the sugar into the bowl, beating for 2–3 minutes or until incorporated and the frosting is smooth and glossy. Refrigerate for 45 minutes, or until firm enough to pipe.

Spread the frosting over the cold cupcakes using a spatula, or spoon the frosting into a piping bag fitted with a star nozzle/tip and pipe it on top of the cupcakes. Top with chopped walnuts.

NOTE
If you can't find crushed pineapple, use canned pineapple chunks, drain and blitz in a food processor. Squeeze out the excess moisture before using.

LOLA'S CHOCOLATE CUPCAKE IS A CLASSIC, MADE TO PERFECTION!
SIMPLE DOESN'T MEAN BORING WHEN YOU HAVE THIS DELICIOUS,
LIGHT AND FLUFFY CHOCOLATE CAKE FINISHED WITH OUR LUXURIOUS
CHOCOLATE BUTTERCREAM.

 # CHOCOLATE

100 g/3½ oz. dark/
    bittersweet chocolate,
    chopped
175 g/1½ sticks butter,
    cubed
225 g/1 cup plus 2
    tablespoons (caster)
    sugar
4 eggs
100 g/¾ cup self-rising
    flour
2½ tablespoons cocoa
    powder
a pinch of salt
sugar stars, to decorate

CHOCOLATE
BUTTERCREAM
135 g/1 stick plus
    1 tablespoon butter,
    cubed and soft
410 g/3 cups icing/
    confectioners' sugar
45 g/⅓ cup cocoa powder
6 tablespoons milk

*muffin pan lined with
    12 muffin cases*

MAKES 12

Preheat the oven to 180°C/350°F/
Gas 4.

Put the chocolate and butter in a
heatproof bowl over a pan of simmering
water. Do not let the base of the bowl
touch the water. Heat, stirring, until the
chocolate melts and you have a smooth,
glossy mixture. Remove from the heat
and stir in the sugar. Let cool for
10 minutes.

Now beat with an electric hand
mixer for 3 minutes. Add the eggs,
one at a time, beating for 10 seconds
between each addition. Sift the flour,
cocoa and salt into the bowl and beat
until blended.

Divide the mixture between the
muffin cases. Bake in the preheated
oven for 20–25 minutes or until well
risen and a skewer inserted in the
middle comes out clean. Remove from
the oven and let cool completely on
a wire rack before decorating.

CHOCOLATE BUTTERCREAM
While the cupcakes are cooling down,
make the chocolate buttercream.

Put the butter in a bowl and beat
with an electric hand mixer until very
soft and smooth. Sift half the sugar and
half the cocoa powder into the bowl,
beating until incorporated. Add the
second half of the sugar and cocoa
and beat on low speed.

Slowly pour in the milk and when
it is mixed in, beat for 3–5 minutes on
a higher speed.

Spread the frosting over the cold
cupcakes using a spatula, or spoon
the frosting into a piping bag fitted with
a star nozzle/tip and pipe it on top of
the cupcakes. Decorate with sugar stars.

LOLA'S VANILLA CUPCAKE IS SPECIAL BECAUSE IT'S MADE USING REAL VANILLA PODS, OR BEANS. YOU CAN TELL THIS FROM THE TINY BLACK SPECKS IN THE CAKE. IT CAN TAKE UP TO THREE YEARS FOR A VANILLA POD TO BE READY TO USE IN COOKING, SO YOU CAN SEE WHY IT'S THE SECOND MOST EXPENSIVE SPICE IN THE WORLD! WE PARTICULARLY LIKE MADAGASCAN VANILLA, BUT TAHITIAN IS MORE FRUITY AND FLORAL.

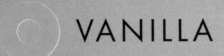

VANILLA

175 g/1⅓ cups plain/
   all-purpose flour
1 teaspoon baking powder
a pinch of salt
150 g/1 stick plus
   2 tablespoons butter,
   cubed and soft
150 g/¾ cup (caster)
   sugar
½ vanilla pod/bean
3 eggs
sugar hearts, butterflies and
   /or flowers, to decorate
edible glitter, to dust

VANILLA BUTTERCREAM
120 g/1 stick butter, cubed
   and soft
500 g/3⅔ cups icing/
   confectioners' sugar
1 teaspoon vanilla extract
1 tablespoon milk
food colouring of your
   choice (optional)

*muffin pan lined with
   12 muffin cases*

MAKES 12

Preheat the oven to 180°C/350°F/Gas 4.

Sift together the flour, baking powder and salt in a bowl.

Put the butter and sugar in a mixing bowl and beat with an electric hand mixer until pale and fluffy. Stop occasionally to scrape down the side of the bowl with a rubber spatula. Using a small, sharp knife, slit the vanilla pod/bean down its length and scrape the seeds out into the mixing bowl. Add the eggs, one at a time, beating well after each addition.

Slowly add the sifted dry ingredients and beat on low speed until combined.

Divide the mixture between the muffin cases. Bake in the preheated oven for 20–25 minutes or until well risen and a skewer inserted in the middle comes out clean. Remove from the oven and let cool completely on a wire rack before decorating.

VANILLA BUTTERCREAM
While the cupcakes are cooling down, make the vanilla buttercream.

Put the butter in a bowl and beat with an electric hand mixer until very soft and smooth. Sift half the sugar into the bowl, beating until incorporated. Add the second half of the sugar and beat on low speed. Add the vanilla. Slowly pour in the milk and when it is mixed in, beat for 3–5 minutes on a higher speed.

Add a few drops of the food colouring of your choice, if using. Beat until evenly incorporated. Refrigerate until required.

Spread the frosting over the cold cupcakes using a spatula, or spoon the frosting into a piping bag fitted with a star nozzle/tip and pipe it on top of the cupcakes. Decorate with sugar hearts, butterflies and/or flowers and dust with edible glitter.

LOLA'S BANANA CUPCAKE IS EASY TO MAKE AND ABSOLUTELY SCRUMPTIOUS. YOU CAN REALLY TASTE THE DELICIOUS SWEETNESS OF THE RIPE BANANAS IN THE LIGHT CAKE, COMPLEMENTED PERFECTLY BY OUR SMOOTH CREAM CHEESE FROSTING. EVEN BETTER, BANANAS CONTAIN VITAMIN B6, VITAMIN C, MANGANESE AND POTASSIUM – MEANING THIS CUPCAKE IS NOT ONLY DELICIOUS BUT GOOD FOR YOU TOO. WELL, ALMOST...

 BANANA

185 g/1½ cups plain/ all-purpose flour
½ teaspoon ground cinnamon
1 teaspoon bicarbonate of/ baking soda
¼ teaspoon salt
2 eggs
200 g/1 cup (caster) sugar
100 ml/scant ½ cup sunflower oil
1 teaspoon vanilla extract
2 large ripe bananas, mashed
dried banana chips, to top
storebought caramel sauce, to drizzle

CREAM CHEESE FROSTING
65 g/½ stick butter, cubed and soft
250 g/8 oz. cream cheese
185 g/1¼ cups icing/ confectioners' sugar

muffin pan lined with 12 muffin cases

MAKES 12

Preheat the oven to 180°C/350°F/ Gas 4.

Sift together the flour, ground cinnamon, bicarbonate of/baking soda and salt in a bowl.

Put the eggs and sugar in a mixing bowl and beat with an electric hand mixer for 5–8 minutes or until thick and pale. Add the oil and vanilla and beat until smooth.

Add the sifted dry ingredients and beat on low speed until combined. Stir in the mashed banana and mix well.

Divide the mixture between the muffin cases. Bake in the preheated oven for 18–20 minutes or until well risen and a skewer inserted in the middle comes out clean. Remove from the oven and let cool completely on a wire rack before decorating.

CREAM CHEESE FROSTING
While the cupcakes are cooling down, make the cream cheese frosting.

Put the butter in a bowl and beat with an electric hand mixer until very soft and smooth. Add the cream cheese and beat on low speed for 2 minutes. Gradually sift the sugar into the bowl, beating for 2–3 minutes or until incorporated and the frosting is smooth and glossy.

Refrigerate for 45 minutes, or until firm enough to pipe.

Spread the frosting over the cold cupcakes using a spatula, or spoon the frosting into a piping bag fitted with a star nozzle/tip and pipe it on top of the cupcakes. Top with dried banana chips and drizzle with caramel sauce.

LOLA'S VANILLA MILK CHOCOLATE CUPCAKE IS SIMPLE TO MAKE AND PROVIDES THE BEST OF BOTH WORLDS – OUR HEAVENLY MADAGASCAN VANILLA CUPCAKE ON THE BOTTOM AND OUR CREAMY-SMOOTH CHOCOLATE BUTTERCREAM ON THE TOP. FOR THE BEST SNOWBALL EFFECT, FINISH THIS CUPCAKE WITH A DRIFT OF CHOCOLATE STRANDS.

 # VANILLA MILK CHOCOLATE

200 g/1½ cups plus 2 tablespoons plain/all-purpose flour
1 teaspoon baking powder
a pinch of salt
175 g/1½ sticks butter, cubed and soft
175 g/¾ cup plus 2 tablespoons (caster) sugar
½ vanilla pod/bean
3 eggs
chocolate vermicelli/jimmies, to decorate
edible glitter, for dusting

CHOCOLATE BUTTERCREAM
135 g/1 stick plus 1 tablespoon butter, cubed and soft
410 g/3 cups icing/confectioners' sugar
45 g/⅓ cup cocoa powder
6 tablespoons milk

muffin pan lined with 12 muffin cases

MAKES 12

Preheat the oven to 180°C/350°F/Gas 4.

Sift together the flour, baking powder and salt in a bowl.

Put the butter and sugar in a mixing bowl and beat with an electric hand mixer until pale and fluffy. Stop occasionally to scrape down the side of the bowl with a rubber spatula. Using a small, sharp knife, slit the vanilla pod/bean down its length and scrape the seeds out into the mixing bowl. Add the eggs, one at a time, beating well after each addition.

Slowly add the sifted dry ingredients and beat on low speed until combined.

Divide the mixture between the muffin cases. Bake in the preheated oven for 20–25 minutes or until well risen and a skewer inserted in the middle comes out clean. Remove from the oven and let cool completely on a wire rack before decorating.

CHOCOLATE BUTTERCREAM

While the cupcakes are cooling down, make the chocolate buttercream.

Put the butter in a bowl and beat with an electric hand mixer until very soft and smooth. Sift half the sugar and half the cocoa powder into the bowl, beating until incorporated. Add the second half of the sugar and cocoa and beat on low speed. Slowly pour in the milk and when it is mixed in, beat for 3–5 minutes on a higher speed.

Spread the frosting over the cold cupcakes using a spatula, making it into a neat dome shape. Pour chocolate vermicelli/jimmies into a saucer and roll the tops of the cupcakes in the sprinkles to completely coat. Finish by dusting with edible glitter.

LOLA'S RED VELVET CUPCAKE IS OUR BESTSELLER BY FAR. IT'S A MILD CHOCOLATE CAKE WITH A BRIGHT RED COLOUR, GARNISHED WITH OUR FAMOUS CREAM CHEESE FROSTING. WE ORIGINALLY CREATED THIS RECIPE TO CELEBRATE THE 4TH JULY, BUT YOU NEED NO EXCUSE TO BAKE THIS CLASSIC ANY TIME OF THE YEAR. WE'VE INCLUDED INSTRUCTIONS FOR AN ULTRA-SIMPLE GLUTEN-FREE VERSION AT THE BOTTOM OF THE PAGE.

RED VELVET

200 g/1½ cups plain/
   all-purpose flour
½ teaspoon baking powder
½ teaspoon bicarbonate
   of/baking soda
1 tablespoon cocoa powder
¼ teaspoon salt
100 g/7 tablespoons
   butter, cubed and soft
175 g/¾ cup (caster) sugar
1 egg, beaten
2 teaspoons red food
   colouring paste
25 g/1 oz. dark/semisweet
   chocolate, melted
2 tablespoons sunflower oil
1 teaspoon white wine
   vinegar
½ teaspoon vanilla extract
120 ml/½ cup single/
   light cream

CREAM CHEESE
FROSTING
65 g/½ stick butter, cubed
   and soft
250 g/8 oz. cream cheese
185 g/1¼ cups icing/
   confectioners' sugar

*muffin pan lined with
   12 muffin cases*

MAKES 12

Preheat the oven to 180°C/350°F/Gas 4.

Sift together the flour, baking powder, bicarbonate of/baking soda, cocoa powder and salt in a bowl.

Put the butter and sugar in a mixing bowl and beat with an electric hand mixer until pale and fluffy. Stop occasionally to scrape down the side of the bowl with a rubber spatula. Slowly beat in the egg, mixing well. Slowly mix in the food colouring. Beat in the melted chocolate, oil, vinegar and vanilla. Gently fold in half the sifted dry ingredients with a large, metal spoon, then half the cream. Repeat with the remaining dry ingredients and cream.

Divide the mixture between the muffin cases. Bake in the preheated oven for 20–25 minutes or until well risen and a skewer inserted in the middle comes out clean. Remove from the oven and let cool completely on a wire rack before decorating.

CREAM CHEESE FROSTING
While the cupcakes are cooling down, make the cream cheese frosting.

Put the butter in a bowl and beat with an electric hand mixer until very soft and smooth. Add the cream cheese and beat on low speed for 2 minutes. Gradually sift the sugar into the bowl, beating for 2–3 minutes or until incorporated and the frosting is smooth and glossy. Refrigerate for 45 minutes, or until firm enough to pipe.

Slice a sliver of cake off the top of each cupcake with a sharp knife. Crumble it between your fingertips to make fine crumbs and set aside.

Spoon the frosting into a piping bag fitted with a star nozzle/tip and pipe it on top of the cupcakes. Pour the reserved crumbs into a saucer and roll the edge of each cupcake in the crumbs to coat.

NOTES
• To make this recipe gluten-free, replace the flour with 190 g/1½ cups rice flour and 3 tablespoons ground almonds and proceed as above.
• Cocoa powder with too high a cocoa content can make the cakes more brown than red. Food colouring paste is available from cake decorating stores.

LOLA'S LEMON CUPCAKE IS SWEET AND TANGY WITH A MOIST, LIGHT TEXTURE. IT IS MADE USING FRESH LEMON ZEST IN BOTH THE CAKE AND BUTTERCREAM. THE DISTINCTIVE SOUR LEMON TASTE MAKES THIS A REFRESHING, MOUTHWATERING CITRUS TREAT. FOR THE BEST FLAVOUR, MAKE SURE YOUR LEMONS ARE FRAGRANT, WITH BRIGHTLY COLOURED YELLOW SKINS.

 # LEMON

225 g/1¾ cups plain/
   all-purpose flour
¾ teaspoon baking powder
¼ teaspoon bicarbonate
   of/baking soda
¼ teaspoon salt
150 g/1 stick plus
   2 tablespoons butter,
   cubed and soft
175 g/¾ cup plus 2
   tablespoons (caster) sugar
3 eggs
2 teaspoons grated lemon
   zest
2 tablespoons lemon juice
100 ml/scant ½ cup milk
yellow sugar crystals, to top

LEMON BUTTERCREAM
125 g/1 stick butter, cubed
   and soft
400 g/3 cups icing/
   confectioners' sugar
1 teaspoon vanilla extract
grated zest of 1 lemon
1 tablespoon milk

*muffin pan lined with
   12 muffin cases*

MAKES 12

Preheat the oven to 180°C/350°F/
Gas 4.

Sift together the flour, baking powder, bicarbonate of/baking soda and salt in a bowl.

Put the butter and sugar in a mixing bowl and beat with an electric hand mixer until pale and fluffy. Stop occasionally to scrape down the side of the bowl with a rubber spatula. Add the eggs, one at a time, beating well after each addition. Beat in the lemon zest and juice.

Gently fold in half the sifted dry ingredients with a large, metal spoon, then half the milk. Repeat with the remaining dry ingredients and milk.

Divide the mixture between the muffin cases. Bake in the preheated oven for 20–25 minutes or until well risen and a skewer inserted in the middle comes out clean. Remove from the oven and let cool completely on a wire rack before decorating.

LEMON BUTTERCREAM
While the cupcakes are cooling down, make the lemon buttercream.

Put the butter in a bowl and beat with an electric hand mixer until very soft and smooth. Sift half the sugar into the bowl, beating until incorporated. Add the second half of the sugar and beat on low speed. Add the vanilla and lemon zest.

Slowly pour in the milk and when it is mixed in, beat for 3–5 minutes on a higher speed.

Spread the frosting over the cold cupcakes using a spatula, or spoon the frosting into a piping bag fitted with a star nozzle/tip and pipe it on top of the cupcakes. Decorate with a cluster of yellow sugar crystals.

LOLA'S ROCKY ROAD CUPCAKE IS A MARBLED VANILLA AND CHOCOLATE CAKE TOPPED WITH OUR SIGNATURE CHOCOLATE BUTTERCREAM. IT IS FINISHED WITH A CONCOCTION OF ALMONDS, CHOCOLATE CHIPS AND MARSHMALLOWS ENROBED IN CHOCOLATE SAUCE. TOTALLY CREAMY, CRUNCHY, CHEWY AND NUTTY!

 # ROCKY ROAD

130 g/1 cup self-rising flour
100 g/¾ cup plain/all-purpose flour
1 teaspoon baking powder
¼ teaspoon salt
130 g/1 stick plus 1 tablespoon butter, cubed and soft
200 g/1 cup (caster) sugar
½ teaspoon vanilla extract
2 eggs
120 ml/½ cup milk
1 tablespoon cocoa powder
3 tablespoons flaked/slivered almonds
25 g/⅓ cup white mini marshmallows
40 g/⅓ cup milk chocolate chips
storebought chocolate sauce, to drizzle

CHOCOLATE BUTTERCREAM
135 g/1 stick plus 1 tablespoon butter, cubed and soft
410 g/3 cups icing/confectioners' sugar
45 g/⅓ cup cocoa powder
6 tablespoons milk

muffin pan lined with 12 muffin cases

MAKES 12

Preheat the oven to 180°C/350°F/Gas 4.

Sift together the flours, baking powder and salt in a bowl.

Put the butter and sugar in a mixing bowl and beat with an electric hand mixer until pale and fluffy. Stop occasionally to scrape down the side of the bowl with a rubber spatula. Add the vanilla. Add the eggs, one at a time, beating well after each addition.

Slowly add the sifted dry ingredients in alternate batches with the milk and beat on low speed until combined.

Transfer half the mixture to another bowl and stir in the cocoa powder.

Scoop 1 tablespoon of the vanilla mixture into each muffin case, followed by 1 tablespoon of the chocolate mixture. Repeat until you have used up all the mixture.

Bake in the preheated oven for 20–25 minutes or until well risen and a skewer inserted in the middle comes out clean. Remove from the oven and let cool completely on a wire rack before decorating.

CHOCOLATE BUTTERCREAM
While the cupcakes are cooling down, make the chocolate buttercream.

Put the butter in a bowl and beat with an electric hand mixer until very soft and smooth. Sift half the sugar and half the cocoa powder into the bowl, beating until incorporated. Add the second half of the sugar and cocoa and beat on low speed.

Slowly pour in the milk and when it is mixed in, beat for 3–5 minutes on a higher speed.

Spread the frosting over the cold cupcakes using a spatula. Cover with the almonds, mini marshmallows and chocolate chips. Finish by drizzling with chocolate sauce.

COOKIES & CREAM IS ONE OF THE BESTSELLING ICE CREAM FLAVOURS IN THE WORLD, SO IT WAS ONLY NATURAL THAT LOLA'S CREATE THE CUPCAKE VERSION. IN ADDITION, WE GET ENDLESS REQUESTS FOR VEGAN CUPCAKES, SO HERE YOU GO! THESE ARE MADE USING CRUSHED VEGAN CHOCOLATE CHIP COOKIES AND THEY ARE ONE OF OUR MOST POPULAR CUPCAKES. THEY'RE SO GOOD, IT WOULD BE A SHAME FOR NON-VEGANS TO MISS OUT!

 # VEGAN COOKIES & CREAM

250 ml/1 cup soya milk
1 teaspoon apple cider vinegar
125 g/1 cup plain/ all-purpose flour
40 g/⅓ cup cocoa powder
¾ teaspoon bicarbonate of/baking soda
½ teaspoon baking powder
a pinch of salt
170 g/¾ cup plus 2 tablespoons (caster) sugar
75 ml/⅓ cup vegetable oil
1½ teaspoons vanilla extract
60 g/2 oz. vegan chocolate chip cookies, plus 6 to decorate

VEGAN 'BUTTERCREAM'
200 g/1 cup soya spread/ natural (soy) buttery spread
1 tablespoon vanilla extract
750 g/5½ cups icing/ confectioners' sugar (see Notes opposite)
about 2–3 tablespoons soya milk

muffin pan lined with 12 muffin cases

MAKES 12

Preheat the oven to 180°C/350°F/ Gas 4.

Mix the soya milk and vinegar together in a bowl and set aside.

Sift the flour, cocoa powder, bicarbonate of/baking soda, baking powder and salt in a mixing bowl.

Add the sugar, oil and vanilla to the soya-milk mixture and beat until foamy. Pour into the dry ingredients in two batches and mix well.

Finally, chop the vegan cookies into small pieces and mix into the cupcake mixture.

Divide the mixture between the muffin cases. Bake in the preheated oven for about 20 minutes or until a skewer inserted in the middle comes out clean. Remove from the oven and let cool completely on a wire rack before decorating.

VEGAN 'BUTTERCREAM'
While the cupcakes are cooling down, make the vegan 'buttercream'.

Put the soya spread/natural buttery spread and vanilla in a mixing bowl. Sift in the sugar. Beat with an electric hand mixer on slow speed until combined, then turn up the speed to medium–high and beat for 2–3 minutes. Add a little milk, if necessary, to loosen.

Spread the frosting over the cold cupcakes using a spatula, or spoon the frosting into a piping bag fitted with a star nozzle/tip and pipe it on top of the cupcakes. Top with half a vegan chocolate chip cookie.

NOTES
• If you like, you can add chopped vegan cookies to the frosting. Make sure the cookies are very finely crushed and mix into the frosting using a spatula. If you want to pipe the frosting, use a piping bag fitted with a large nozzle/tip so that the cookie crumbs don't get stuck in the tip.
• Most icing/confectioners' sugar is vegan, but check the packaging before you buy. If in doubt, look for organic icing/confectioners' sugar, which tends to be vegan-friendly.
• Vegan-friendly ingredients are available at most health-food stores or major supermarkets.

LOLA'S CHOCOLATE MILK IS OUR VERSION OF THE COLD, COCOA-FLAVOURED MILK DRINK. IT COMBINES OUR LIGHT, FLUFFY AND MOIST CHOCOLATEY CUPCAKE WITH OUR DELICIOUS VANILLA MILKY BUTTERCREAM. SIMPLE TO MAKE AND SUPER CREAMY FOR AN ULTRA-DELICIOUS AFTERNOON TREAT.

 # CHOCOLATE MILK

100 g/3½ oz. dark/ bittersweet chocolate, chopped
175 g/1½ sticks butter, cubed
225 g/1 cup plus 2 tablespoons (caster) sugar
4 eggs
100 g/¾ cup self-rising flour
2½ tablespoons cocoa powder
a pinch of salt
chocolate sprinkles, to top
edible glitter, to dust

VANILLA BUTTERCREAM
120 g/1 stick butter, cubed and soft
500 g/3⅔ cups icing/ confectioners' sugar
1 teaspoon vanilla extract
1 tablespoon milk

muffin pan lined with 12 muffin cases

MAKES 12

Preheat the oven to 180°C/350°F/ Gas 4.

Put the chocolate and butter in a heatproof bowl over a pan of simmering water. Do not let the base of the bowl touch the water. Heat, stirring, until the chocolate melts and you have a smooth, glossy mixture. Remove from the heat and stir in the sugar. Let cool for 10 minutes.

Now beat with an electric hand mixer for 3 minutes. Add the eggs, one at a time, beating for 10 seconds between each addition. Sift the flour, cocoa and salt into the bowl and beat until blended.

Divide the mixture between the muffin cases. Bake in the preheated oven for 20–25 minutes or until well risen and a skewer inserted in the middle comes out clean. Remove from the oven and let cool completely on a wire rack before decorating.

VANILLA BUTTERCREAM
While the cupcakes are cooling down, make the vanilla buttercream.

Put the butter in a bowl and beat with an electric hand mixer until very soft and smooth. Sift half the sugar into the bowl, beating until incorporated. Add the second half of the sugar and beat on low speed. Add the vanilla. Slowly pour in the milk and when it is mixed in, beat for 3–5 minutes on a higher speed.

Spread the frosting over the cold cupcakes using a spatula, or spoon the frosting into a piping bag fitted with a star nozzle/tip and pipe it on top of the cupcakes. Decorate with chocolate sprinkles and dust with edible glitter.

ORIGINALLY CREATED IN HONOUR OF THE 27,000 KG/59,500 LBS OF STRAWBERRIES EATEN EVERY YEAR AT THE WIMBLEDON TENNIS CHAMPIONSHIPS, THIS IS ANOTHER CUPCAKE THAT WAS TOO GOOD NOT TO BAKE EVERY DAY OF THE YEAR AT LOLA'S. DELICIOUS FRESH STRAWBERRIES ARE SWIRLED WITH WHITE CHOCOLATE IN THE CAKE MIXTURE, MAKING THIS A SENSATIONALLY INDULGENT TREAT.

 # STRAWBERRY

210 g/1⅔ cups self-rising flour
1 teaspoon baking powder
a pinch of salt
90 g/6 tablespoons butter
150 g/¾ cup (caster) sugar
2 teaspoons lemon juice
grated zest of ½ lemon
2 eggs
80 ml/⅓ cup single/light cream
120 g/4 oz. white chocolate, grated
120 g/1 cup strawberries, roughly chopped, plus 12 whole strawberries, to decorate

STRAWBERRY BUTTERCREAM
120 g/1 stick butter, cubed and soft
500 g/3⅔ cups icing/confectioners' sugar
1 teaspoon vanilla extract
1 tablespoon milk
4 strawberries

muffin pan lined with 12 muffin cases

MAKES 12

Sift together the flour, baking powder and salt in a bowl.

Put the butter and sugar in a mixing bowl and beat with an electric hand mixer until pale and fluffy. Stop occasionally to scrape down the side of the bowl with a rubber spatula. Add the lemon juice and zest. Add the eggs, one at a time, beating well after each addition.

Pour in one third of the sifted dry ingredients and beat on low speed. Add half the cream and beat well. Repeat this process, then finish with the last third of the dry ingredients. Finally, fold in the grated chocolate and chopped strawberries.

Divide the mixture between the muffin cases. Bake in the preheated oven for 20–25 minutes or until well risen and a skewer inserted in the middle comes out clean. Remove from the oven and let cool completely on a wire rack before decorating.

STRAWBERRY BUTTERCREAM
While the cupcakes are cooling down, make the strawberry buttercream.

Put the butter in a bowl and beat with an electric hand mixer until very soft and smooth. Sift half the sugar into the bowl, beating until incorporated. Add the second half of the sugar and beat on low speed. Add the vanilla. Slowly pour in the milk and beat.

Mash the strawberries with a fork or potato masher until well puréed. Beat into the buttercream and when they are mixed in, beat for 3–5 minutes on a higher speed. Refrigerate for 1–2 hours, or until firm enough to pipe.

Spread the frosting over the cold cupcakes using a spatula, or spoon the frosting into a piping bag fitted with a star nozzle/tip and pipe it on top of the cupcakes. Top with a strawberry.

LOLA'S COCONUT & LIME CUPCAKE IS A MATCH MADE IN A TROPICAL PARADISE! THE CAKE IS BURSTING WITH LIME ZEST AND IS INCREDIBLY MOIST. IT IS DECORATED WITH A LIME BUTTERCREAM AND GORGEOUS COCONUT FLAKES, PROVIDING A WONDERFUL BALANCE OF FLAVOURS. PICTURE YOURSELF SITTING UNDER A COCONUT TREE ENJOYING YOUR COCONUT & LIME LOLA'S FOR A TRULY EXOTIC EXPERIENCE.

 # COCONUT & LIME

220 g/1¾ cups plain/
    all-purpose flour
1 teaspoon baking powder
1 teaspoon bicarbonate of/
    baking soda
grated zest of 1 lime, plus
    12 lime slices to decorate
70 g/½ cup desiccated
    coconut
110 g/7 tablespoons
    butter, melted
1 teaspoon honey
130 g/⅔ cup (caster) sugar
175 ml/¾ cup coconut
    water
175 ml/¾ cup milk
coconut flakes, to decorate

LIME BUTTERCREAM
120 g/1 stick butter, cubed
    and soft
500 g/3⅔ cups icing/
    confectioners' sugar
1 teaspoon vanilla extract
grated zest of ½ lime
2 teaspoons lime juice
1 tablespoon milk

*muffin pan lined with
    12 muffin cases*

MAKES 12

Preheat the oven to 180°C/350°F/
Gas 4.

Sift together the flour, baking powder and bicarbonate of/baking soda in a bowl. Stir in the lime zest and desiccated coconut.

Put the melted butter, honey and sugar in a mixing bowl and beat in the coconut water and milk using an electric hand mixer until combined.

Add the dry ingredients and beat on low speed until well mixed.

Divide the mixture between the muffin cases. Bake in the preheated oven for 20–25 minutes or until well risen and a skewer inserted in the middle comes out clean. Remove from the oven and let cool completely on a wire rack before decorating.

LIME BUTTERCREAM
While the cupcakes are cooling down, make the lime buttercream.

Put the butter in a bowl and beat with an electric hand mixer until very soft and smooth. Sift half the sugar into the bowl, beating until incorporated. Add the second half of the sugar and beat on low speed. Add the vanilla, lime zest and juice. Slowly pour in the milk and when it is mixed in, beat for 3–5 minutes on a higher speed.

Spread the frosting over the cold cupcakes using a spatula. Cover with coconut flakes and top with a twisted slice of lime.

NOTE
There are no eggs in this recipe.

LOLA'S PEANUT BUTTER CUPCAKE IS MADE USING SMOOTH PEANUT BUTTER BOTH INSIDE THE CAKE MIXTURE AND IN THE BUTTERCREAM. ALTHOUGH IT'S HARD TO BEAT AS A SANDWICH SPREAD, GOOEY PEANUT BUTTER INSIDE A CUPCAKE IS DEFINITELY SOMETHING TO TRY AT LEAST ONCE! ORIGINALLY CREATED TO CELEBRATE NATIONAL PEANUT BUTTER DAY ON 24 JANUARY, THIS CUPCAKE HAS BEEN A HUGE HIT (ESPECIALLY WITH JAMES, OUR BEST 'PB' CUSTOMER!) AND IT IS NOW BAKED EVERY DAY AT LOLA'S.

PEANUT BUTTER

150 g/1⅓ cups plain/
    all-purpose flour
1 teaspoon baking powder
125 g/1 stick butter, cubed
    and soft
150 g/¾ cup packed dark
    brown sugar
1 teaspoon vanilla extract
165 g/⅔ cup smooth
    all-natural peanut butter
1 large egg
110 ml/scant ½ cup milk
chopped peanuts and
    12 Reese's Peanut Butter
    Cups, to decorate

PEANUT BUTTERCREAM
200 g/1⅔ sticks butter,
    cubed and soft
400 g/3 cups icing/
    confectioners' sugar
3 tablespoons milk
115 g/½ cup smooth
    all-natural peanut butter

*muffin pan lined with
    12 muffin cases*

MAKES 12

Preheat the oven to 180°C/350°F/ Gas 4.

Sift together the flour and baking powder in a bowl.

Put the butter, sugar and vanilla in a mixing bowl and beat with an electric hand mixer until pale and fluffy. Stop occasionally to scrape down the side of the bowl with a rubber spatula. Add the peanut butter and beat again. Gradually beat in the egg.

Fold in the sifted dry ingredients and milk alternately.

Divide the mixture between the muffin cases. Bake in the preheated oven for 20–25 minutes or until well risen and a skewer inserted in the middle comes out clean. Remove from the oven and let cool completely on a wire rack before decorating.

PEANUT BUTTERCREAM
While the cupcakes are cooling down, make the peanut buttercream.

Put the butter in a bowl and beat with an electric hand mixer until very soft and smooth. Sift half the sugar into the bowl, beating until incorporated and the frosting is smooth.

Add the second half of the sugar, as well as the milk and beat for 3–5 minutes until the buttercream is thick and creamy. Finally, fold in the peanut butter.

Spread the frosting over the cold cupcakes using a spatula, or spoon the frosting into a piping bag fitted with a star nozzle/tip and pipe it on top of the cupcakes. Decorate with chopped peanuts and halved Reese's Peanut Butter Cups.

LOLA'S BANANA CHOCOLATE CUPCAKE BRINGS TOGETHER OUR FAVOURITE FLAVOUR COMBINATIONS. IT COMBINES THE SWEETNESS OF RIPE, MASHED BANANAS WITH A DELICIOUS COCOA POWDER IN OUR CHOCOLATEY BUTTERCREAM. BANANAS AND CHOCOLATE ARE USED TOGETHER IN SO MANY TREATS – THE 'BANANA BOAT' STUFFED WITH CHOCOLATE AND MARSHMALLOWS AND EATEN BY THE CAMPFIRE IN THE USA AND, MOST FAMOUSLY, THE BANANA SPLIT, WITH CHOCOLATE ICE CREAM AND SYRUP. HEALTHY AND DELICIOUS DON'T ALWAYS GO TOGETHER, BUT THIS ONE IS A WINNER!

 # BANANA CHOCOLATE

230 g/1¾ cups plus 1 tablespoon self-rising flour
1 teaspoon ground cinnamon
2 eggs
200 g/1 cup (caster) sugar
100 g/½ cup vegetable oil
1 teaspoon vanilla extract
2 ripe bananas, mashed, plus 12 slices to decorate
1½ tablespoons warm milk
1 teaspoon baking powder
100 g/¾ cup pecans
chocolate sprinkles, to top

CHOCOLATE BUTTERCREAM
135 g/1 stick plus 1 tablespoon butter, cubed and soft
410 g/3 cups icing/ confectioners' sugar
45 g/⅓ cup cocoa powder
6 tablespoons milk

muffin pan lined with 12 muffin cases

MAKES 12

Preheat the oven to 190°C/375°F/ Gas 5.

Sift together the flour and ground cinnamon in a bowl.

Put the eggs and sugar in a mixing bowl and beat with an electric hand mixer for 5–8 minutes or until thick and pale. Add the oil and vanilla and beat until smooth. Add the mashed bananas and beat on low speed until combined.

Mix the warm milk and baking powder together, then beat into the banana mixture. Gradually beat in the sifted dry ingredients and beat on low speed until combined. Finally, chop the pecans and fold them into the mixture.

Divide the mixture between the muffin cases. Bake in the preheated oven for about 25 minutes or until well risen and a skewer inserted in the middle comes out clean. Remove from the oven and let cool completely on a wire rack before decorating.

CHOCOLATE BUTTERCREAM
While the cupcakes are cooling down, make the chocolate buttercream.

Put the butter in a bowl and beat with an electric hand mixer until very soft and smooth.

Sift half the sugar and half the cocoa powder into the bowl, beating until incorporated. Add the second half of the sugar and cocoa and beat on low speed.

Slowly pour in the milk and when it is mixed in, beat for 3–5 minutes on a higher speed.

Spread the frosting over the cold cupcakes using a spatula, or spoon the frosting into a piping bag fitted with a star nozzle/tip and pipe it on top of the cupcakes.

Pour chocolate sprinkles into a saucer and roll the edge of each cupcake in the sprinkles to coat. Top with a slice of banana.

INDEX

ACKNOWLEDGMENTS

The real thank you goes to our parents and families, as without their knowledge, support, love and bold taste-testing we would never have been able to grow LOLA's as quickly and successfully as we did. They've really seen it all and never doubted our dreams – this book is testament to their continued belief in us. Thank you from the bottom of our hearts.

We are eternally grateful to our entire extraordinary team at LOLA's – decorators, bakers, delivery drivers, office staff, store managers and retail assistants. You continue to amaze us with your creative spirit, dedication and passion for this business. Specifically we would like to thank Terri Gibson and Keith Irish Waters for ensuring every recipe in the book is absolutely perfect. Nicole Goss, Katheryne Goosby, Polly Thompson, Megan Lewis-Thomas for your organisation, collaborative spirit and brilliant ideas. Marietta Tovera and Carol Lanigan for all your assistance and guidance in the very early days. Kirsten Smith for helping us to translate our story into words. Jane Milton, Cecilia Edmunds and your team of fabulous testers for all your dedication and commitment to this project.

Special thanks to Alison Starling, Céline Hughes, Leslie Harrington, Megan Smith, Lauren Wright, Kate Whitaker, Cindy Richards, Lucy McKelvie, Liz Belton and all the team at Ryland Peters & Small for giving us the opportunity to write this book, for being so enthusiastic and supportive and for creating a beautiful book that remains true to the LOLA's brand and ethos.

To our customers, you are our inspiration and we thank you all for your continued support and commitment to LOLA's.

And a huge thank you to everyone else we have met and worked with on this journey. We look forward to the next chapter…